300·72 FLI

ITEM NO: 1889242

KT-452-247

Designing Qualitative Research

UNIVERSITY OF WALES, NEWPORT

LIBRARY
AND
INFORMATION
SERVICES
CAERLEON

Designing Qualitative Research (by Uwe Flick) is the first part of *The Sage Qualitative Research Kit*. This *Kit* comprises eight books and taken together the *Kit* represents the most extensive and detailed introduction to the process of doing qualitative research. This book can be used in conjuction with other titles in the *Kit* as part of this overall introduction to qualitative methods but this book can equally well be used on its own as an introduction to designing qualitative research.

Complete list of titles in *The SAGE Qualitative Research Kit*

- Designing Qualitative Research *Uwe Flick*
- Doing Interviews *Steinar Kvale*
- Doing Ethnographic and Observational Research *Michael Angrosino*
- Doing Focus Groups *Rosaline Barbour*
- Using Visual Data in Qualitative Research *Marcus Banks*
- Analysing Qualitative Data *Graham R. Gibbs*
- Doing Conversation, Discourse and Document Analysis *Tim Rapley*
- Managing Quality in Qualitative Research *Uwe Flick*

Members of the Editorial Advisory Board

Juliet Corbin	San Jose State University, Oakland, USA
Norman K. Denzin	University of Illinois, Urbana Champaign, USA
Peter Freebody	University of Queensland, S. Lucia, Australia
Ken Gergen	Swarthmore College, Swarthmore, USA
Jennifer Mason	Manchester University, Manchester, UK
Michael Murray	Keele University, Keele, UK
Clive Seale	Brunel University, Uxbridge, UK
Jonathan Potter	Loughborough University, Loughborough, UK
Margaret Wetherell	Open University, Milton Keynes, UK

Designing Qualitative Research

Uwe Flick

SAGE Publications
Los Angeles • London • New Delhi • Singapore

© Uwe Flick 2007

First published 2007

Apart from any fair dealing for the purposes of research or private
study, or criticism or review, as permitted under the Copyright,
Designs and Patents Act, 1988, this publication may be reproduced,
stored or transmitted in any form, or by any means, only with the
prior permission in writing of the publishers, or in the case of
reprographic reproduction, in accordance with the terms of licences
issued by the Copyright Licensing Agency. Enquiries concerning
reproduction outside those terms should be sent to the publishers.

SAGE Publications Ltd
1 Oliver's Yard
55 City Road
London EC1Y 1SP

SAGE Publications Inc.
2455 Teller Road
Thousand Oaks, California 91320

SAGE Publications India Pvt Ltd
B 1/I 1 Mohan Cooperative Industrial Area
Mathura Road, New Delhi 110 044
India

SAGE Publications Asia-Pacific Pte Ltd
33 Pekin Street #02-01
Far East Square
Singapore 048763

Library of Congress Control Number: 2006938283

British Library Cataloguing in Publication data

A catalogue record for this book is available from the British Library

ISBN 978-0-7619-4976-3

Typeset by C&M Digitals (P) Ltd, Chennai, India
Printed in Great Britain by The Cromwell Press Ltd, Trowbridge, Wiltshire
Printed on paper from sustainable resources

▐▐▐ Contents

▌▌▌ List of illustrations

Boxes

Figures

Tables

Editorial introduction
Uwe Flick

- Introduction to *The SAGE Qualitative Research Kit*
- What is qualitative research?
- How do we conduct qualitative research?
- Scope of *The SAGE Qualitative Research Kit*

Introduction to *The SAGE Qualitative Research Kit*

In recent years, qualitative research has enjoyed a period of unprecedented growth and diversification as it has become an established and respected research approach across a variety of disciplines and contexts. An increasing number of students, teachers and practitioners are facing questions and problems of how to do qualitative research – in general and for their specific individual purposes. To answer these questions, and to address such practical problems on a how-to-do level, is the main purpose of *The SAGE Qualitative Research Kit*.

The books in *The SAGE Qualitative Research Kit* collectively address the core issues that arise when we actually do qualitative research. Each book focuses on key methods (e.g. interviews or focus groups) or materials (e.g. visual data or discourse) that are used for studying the social world in qualitative terms. Moreover, the books in the *Kit* have been written with the needs of many different types of reader in mind. As such, the *Kit* and the individual books will be of use to a wide variety of users:

- *Practitioners* of qualitative research in the social sciences, medical research, marketing research, evaluation, organizational, business and management studies, cognitive science, etc., who face the problem of planning and conducting a specific study using qualitative methods.
- *University teachers* and lecturers in these fields using qualitative methods will be expected to use these series as a basis of their teaching.

- *Undergraduate and graduate students* of social sciences, nursing, education, psychology and other fields where qualitative methods are a (main) part of the university training including practical applications (e.g. for writing a thesis).

Each book in *The SAGE Qualitative Research Kit* has been written by a distinguished author with extensive experience in their field and in the practice with methods they write about. When reading the whole series of books from the beginning to the end, you will repeatedly come across some issues which are central to any sort of qualitative research – such as ethics, designing research or assessing quality. However, in each book such issues are addressed from the specific methodological angle of the authors and the approach they describe. Thus you may find different approaches to issues of quality or different suggestions of how to analyze qualitative data in the different books, which will combine to present a comprehensive picture of the field as a whole.

What is qualitative research?

It has become more and more difficult to find a common definition of qualitative research which is accepted by the majority of qualitative research approaches and researchers. Qualitative research is no longer just simply '*not quantitative research*', but has developed an identity (or maybe multiple identities) of its own.

Despite the multiplicity of approaches to qualitative research, some common features of qualitative research can be identified. Qualitative research is intended to approach the world 'out there' (not in specialized research settings such as laboratories) and to understand, describe and sometimes explain social phenomena 'from the inside' in a number of different ways:

- By analyzing experiences of individuals or groups. Experiences can be related to biographical life histories or to (everyday or professional) practices; they may be addressed by analyzing everyday knowledge, accounts and stories.
- By analyzing interactions and communications in the making. This can be based on observing or recording practices of interacting and communicating and analyzing this material.
- By analyzing documents (texts, images, film or music) or similar traces of experiences or interactions.

Common to such approaches is that they seek to unpick how people construct the world around them, what they are doing or what is happening to them in terms that are meaningful and that offer rich insight. Interactions and documents are seen as ways of constituting social processes and artefacts collaboratively (or conflictingly). All of these approaches represent ways of meaning, which can be reconstructed and analyzed with different qualitative methods that allow the researcher to develop (more or less generalizable) models, typologies, theories as ways of describing and explaining social (or psychological) issues.

How do we conduct qualitative research?

Can we identify common ways of doing qualitative research if we take into account that there are different theoretical, epistemological and methodological approaches to qualitative research and that the issues that are studied are very diverse as well? We can at least identify some common features of how qualitative research is done.

- Qualitative researchers are interested in accessing experiences, interactions and documents in their natural context and in a way that gives room to the particularities of them and the materials in which they are studied.
- Qualitative research refrains from setting up a well-defined concept of what is studied and from formulating hypotheses in the beginning in order to test them. Rather, concepts (or hypotheses, if they are used) are developed and refined in the process of research.
- Qualitative research starts from the idea that methods and theories should be appropriate to what is studied. If the existing methods do not fit to a concrete issue or field, they are adapted or new methods or approaches are developed.
- Researchers themselves are an important part of the research process, either in terms of their own personal presence as researchers, or in terms of their experiences in the field and with the reflexivity they bring to the role – as are members of the field under study.
- Qualitative research takes context and cases seriously for understanding an issue under study. A lot of qualitative research is based on case studies or a series of case studies, and often the case (its history and complexity) is an important context for understanding what is studied.
- A major part of qualitative research is based on text and writing – from field notes and transcripts to descriptions and interpretations and finally to the presentation of the findings and of the research as a whole. Therefore, issues of transforming complex social situations (or other materials such as images) into texts – issues of transcribing and writing in general – are major concerns of qualitative research.
- If methods are supposed to be adequate to what is under study, approaches to defining and assessing the quality of qualitative research (still) have to be discussed in specific ways that are appropriate for qualitative research and even for specific approaches in qualitative research.

Scope of *The SAGE Qualitative Research Kit*

- *Designing Qualitative Research* (Uwe Flick) gives a brief introduction to qualitative research from the point of view of how to plan and design a concrete study using qualitative research in one way or the other. It is intended to outline a framework for the other books in *The Sage Qualitative Research Kit* by focusing on how-to-do problems and on how to solve such problems in the research process. The book will address issues of constructing a research design in qualitative research; it will outline stepping-stones in making a research project work and will discuss practical problems such as resources in qualitative research but also more methodological issues like quality of qualitative research and also ethics. This framework is spelled out in more details in the other books in the *Kit*.
- Three books are devoted to collecting or producing data in qualitative research. They take up the issues briefly outlined in the first book and approach them in a much more detailed and focused way for the specific method. First, *Doing Interviews* (Steinar Kvale) addresses the theoretical, epistemological, ethical and practical issues of interviewing people about specific issues or their life history. *Doing Ethnographic and Observational Research* (Michael Angrosino) focuses on the second major approach to collecting and producing qualitative data. Here again practical issues (like selecting sites, methods of collecting data in ethnography, special problems of analyzing them) are discussed in the context of more general issues (ethics, representations, quality and adequacy of ethnography as an approach). In *Doing Focus Groups* (Rosaline Barbour) the third of the most important qualitative methods of producing data is presented. Here again we find a strong focus on how-to-do issues of sampling, designing and analyzing the data and on how to produce them in focus groups.
- Three further volumes are devoted to analyzing specific types of qualitative data. *Using Visual Data in Qualitative Research* (Marcus Banks) extends the focus to the third type of qualitative data (beyond verbal data coming from interviews and focus groups and observational data). The use of visual data has not only become a major trend in social research in general, but confronts researchers with new practical problems in using them and analyzing them and produces new ethical issues. In *Analyzing Qualitative Data* (Graham R. Gibbs), several practical approaches and issues of making sense of any sort of qualitative data are addressed. Special attention is paid to practices of coding, of comparing and of using computer-assisted qualitative data analysis. Here, the focus is on verbal data like interviews, focus groups or biographies. *Doing Conversation, Discourse and Document Analysis* (Tim Rapley) extends this focus to different types of data, relevant for analyzing discourses. Here, the focus is on existing material (like documents) and on recording everyday

conversations and on finding traces of discourses. Practical issues such as generating an archive, transcribing video materials and of how to analyze discourses with such types of data are discussed.

- *Managing Quality in Qualitative Research* (Uwe Flick) takes up the issue of quality in qualitative research, which has been briefly addressed in specific contexts in other books in the *Kit*, in a more general way. Here, quality is looked at from the angle of using or reformulating existing or defining new criteria for qualitative research. This book will examine the ongoing debates about what should count as defining 'quality' and validity in qualitative methodologies and will examine the many strategies for promoting and managing quality in qualitative research. Special attention is paid to the strategy of triangulation in qualitative research and to the use of quantitative research in the context of promoting the quality of qualitative research.

Before I go on to outline the focus of this book and its role in the *Kit*, I would like to thank some people at SAGE who were important in making this *Kit* happen. Michael Carmichael suggested this project to me some time ago and was very helpful with his suggestions in the beginning. Patrick Brindle took over and continued this support, as did Vanessa Harwood and Jeremy Toynbee in making books out of the manuscripts we provided.

About this book
Uwe Flick

In qualitative research, the issue of designing research is not as prominent as it is in quantitative approaches. Nevertheless, qualitative research should be planned as well and there are several decisions to take along the way in the research process: formulating a research question, deciding about sampling, thinking of how to generalize and to which aim and the like. These are issues and decisions that influence the design of a qualitative study. However, they may arise in different forms depending on what kind of research is planned in detail. Sampling for an interview is different from constructing a group in focus group research. Selecting sites and people in ethnography is different from taking a sample from an archive of photos or documents. Such issues will be taken up in the books of Barbour (2007) or Angrosino (2007) with a specific perspective on the single method.

Compared to that, this book has a more general focus than the other books in *The SAGE Qualitative Research Kit*. Thus, design issues will be discussed here from different angles and they will be discussed in more detail again in the other books of *The SAGE Qualitative Research Kit*. This book adds a more comparative perspective on research designs in qualitative research to the more specific one taken in the other books. It will address sampling, for example, on different levels (of people, of sites, of documents or inside materials, interviews and the like). It will also focus on how research questions are developed from more general research interests and personal or political backgrounds. Resources and stepping-stones in making qualitative research work will also be an issue. In dealing with these issues, the book has a more specific approach than the other books in *The SAGE Qualitative Research Kit* as it takes research designs as the specific approach for introducing the readers to qualitative research. In this sense, the book has two functions in the context of *The SAGE Qualitative Research Kit*: as a stand-alone book it aims at giving a comprehensive account of the problems and solutions in the field of designing qualitative research; as an addition to the other books in the *Kit*, it rounds up the framework for the other books on a practical and on a methodological level.

1
What is qualitative research?

Chapter objectives
After reading this chapter, you should

- see common features of qualitative research and its proliferation at the same time;
- know about the research perspectives and the role of theory in qualitative research; and
- understand that qualitative research is located in the tension of methods and attitudes.

Defining qualitative research

The term 'qualitative research' was for a long time used in a distinctive way to describe an alternative to 'quantitative' research and was coined against the background of a critique of the latter and especially the development it had taken in the 1960s and 1970s. However, qualitative research has a long history in many disciplines, where social research in general began with approaches that would now be summarized under qualitative research. The longer the development proceeded, the more a profile of what was meant by this term became clear. This profile is no longer defined *ex negativo* – qualitative research is *not* quantitative or *not* standardized or the like – but it is characterized by several features. Thus, qualitative research uses text as empirical material (instead of numbers), starts from the notion of the social construction of realities under study, is interested in the perspectives of participants, in everyday practices and everyday knowledge referring to the issue under study. Methods should be appropriate to that issue and should be open enough to allow an understanding of a process or relation (see Flick, 2006, for more detail). Does this mean that we can see a common understanding of what qualitative research is? In the latest edition of their handbook, Denzin and Lincoln offer an 'initial, generic definition':

> Qualitative research is a situated activity that locates the observer in the world. It consists of a set of interpretive, material practices that make the world visible. These practices transform the world. They turn the world into a series of representations, including field notes, interviews, conversations, photographs, recordings, and memos to the self. At this level, qualitative research involves an interpretive, naturalistic approach to the world. This means that qualitative researchers study things in their natural settings, attempting to make sense of, or interpret, phenomena in terms of the meanings people bring to them. (2005a, p. 3)

This seems to be a good definition of what qualitative research is about. Nevertheless, if you take conversation analysis as an example (see Rapley, 2007, or Ten Have, 1999), researchers are interested in the formal organization of talk about something and not in the meanings people bring to a phenomenon. Nevertheless, conversation analysis is a prominent example of qualitative research. A lot of qualitative research starts from a 'naturalistic approach to the world' and a great deal of qualitative research has an interpretive approach to it. But in many contexts, both are seen as something different on the levels of epistemology and methodology, which makes it difficult to simply combine 'interpretive naturalistic' in one approach. These remarks are not so much meant as a critique of Denzin and Lincoln's definition; rather, to thus demonstrate the difficulties in formulating such a definition as a *generic* definition.

Proliferation of qualitative research

Qualitative research has been developing for a long time now. The label 'qualitative research' is used as an umbrella term for a series of approaches to research in the social sciences. These are also known as hermeneutic, reconstructive or interpretive approaches (see Flick, 2006, and Flick et al., 2004a, for recent overviews). Also, sometimes the term 'inquiry' is preferred to 'research' or both are given up for naming the whole enterprise as 'ethnography'. Nevertheless, under the label of qualitative research, these approaches and methods and the results obtained by using them are attracting increasing attention not only in sociology, but also in education, psychology, health sciences and the like. In some of these areas, special handbooks of qualitative research (in psychology, for example) are published and at the same time hardly any handbook (in rehabilitation, nursing science or public health, for instance) is published today that does not have a chapter on qualitative research methods. Without going into details of a history of qualitative research here, we can notice a success story. Indicators for that are the growing numbers of special journals for qualitative research or of established journals opening up for qualitative research to be published. The number of textbooks, handbooks, monographs and edited books is constantly increasing and in many areas the part of qualitative research in funded research is growing considerably. Also, the number of courses and curricula dedicated to qualitative research is growing. Finally, an increasing number of young researchers do their master or doctoral thesis against the background of a study using qualitative or a combination of qualitative and quantitative methods. All these indicators of a success story of qualitative research maybe differ in their relevance in various disciplines and in different countries. But they describe an overall trend of establishing qualitative research as an approach that is taken seriously in more and more contexts.

At the same time, we cannot see that this trend of establishing qualitative research is accompanied by developing something like a paradigmatic core of what qualitative research is. Although some overall principles can be identified (see above), we are confronted by a continuous proliferation of qualitative research on – at least – four levels:

- First of all, there are different research programs in qualitative research, which have different issues of research, specific methods and theoretical backgrounds. Examples may be grounded theory research or discourse analysis, which have different interests and methodological principles, but are both prominent in qualitative research.
- Second, we can see differences in what is understood as qualitative research in the US, in the UK, or for example in Germany (see Knoblauch et al., 2005, for such a comparative view on qualitative research in different countries). The first proliferation of course is also relevant inside each of these national traditions. The Denzin and Lincoln definition and their handbook, for example, basically represent the discussion in the US.
- Third, we find different discourses about qualitative research in different disciplines. Qualitative researchers in psychology have specific interests and problems, as do their colleagues in sociology for example, but both are not necessarily the same.
- Fourth, we see a growing diversity of area-specific discourses about qualitative research. Examples are contracted qualitative research in health sciences or in management or in evaluation. These areas have their special needs and limitations, which are different from, for example, university research in the context of master or doctoral theses or in the context of 'basic' research.

3

Someone who expects the development of standards for qualitative research from a long history of research and methodological discussion may be puzzled or disappointed by this proliferation. At some points this may produce problems in the acceptance of qualitative research and weaken its position in the competition with quantitative researchers, when funding resources are to be allocated. However, this proliferation can also be seen as characteristic for qualitative research due to one of its main features – or guiding principles – of all sorts of qualitative research.

Appropriateness as guiding principle

The development of qualitative research is linked to the principle of appropriateness in three ways. Originally, at the beginning of empirical research in several disciplines, there were more issues to be studied than methods to use. We can trace back how the methods used in early studies of qualitative research were developed out of a specific knowledge interest on the one hand and of the features of what should be studied on the other hand. Vidich and Lyman (2000) show how the methods of early ethnography were informed by the researchers' interests in 'the Other', which at that time meant understanding the difference between non-Western cultures and the researchers' own Western backgrounds. This was then extended to comparative approaches describing different versions of cultures from a comparative and evolutionary point of view and later on applied to understanding and describing specific parts of one's own culture in the studies of the Chicago School, for example. Another example is the development of Piaget's research methods from his interest in understanding children's development and thinking in different stages. In this phase of the development, the need for appropriateness of the methods in (what was later called) qualitative research resulted from the characteristics of the issues that were discovered for research and from the lack of a developed methodology ready to be applied in such studies (see also Flick, 2006, chap. 1, for a brief history of qualitative research).

A second link to appropriateness as a principle can be identified much later in the renaissance of qualitative research in the 1960s and 1970s. Here we find a different situation: methodologies had been developed, established, and refined. Disciplines had linked their own development and establishment to a specific method – the experiment in psychology, the use of surveys in sociology, for example. For the latter, this was complemented by the development of 'grand theories' (like the ones of Talcott Parsons for example) to describe how societies function in general and in detail. At the same time, both methods and theories missed a growing number of issues that were practically relevant, but more small-scale and difficult to understand. As a result of such developments, a lack of methods (and theories) ready to describe and explain relevant phenomena led to a rediscovery of qualitative research. Examples of how the lack of adequate, appropriate methods has led to creating new methods and research programs for developing empirically 'grounded theories' are the studies of Erving Goffman

(1959) or Howard Becker, Anselm Strauss and Barney Glaser (Becker et al., 1961). They were interested in using empirical research for discovering and developing theories of practically relevant phenomena, which could not be addressed by surveys or grand theories. In this phase, the principle of appropriateness became relevant for qualitative research because of the gap between established methodologies and the issues that could not be studied adequately with these methodologies. The principle of appropriateness led to the development of a range of qualitative methods – sometimes to a rediscovery and further development of already existing methods – of research programs and of an extended methodological discourse of qualitative research. For this phase, again, we can trace back methodological features of qualitative research methods (and programs) to the features of the issues that were studied.

In a third sense, the principle of appropriateness has become relevant in the current situation. Now, we can notice a further proliferation of qualitative research in a variety of research areas. If we have a look at areas like organization studies or management research, at fields like health research in general or nursing research in particular, we find specific features of the fields and issues to be studied. These have led to developing methodological discourses that are specific and different from the discourse in qualitative research in general. Management research, for example, is confronted with very specific structures (of organizations). Nursing research often works with people in a very specific situation – the vulnerability of patients or of their relatives confronted with illness and death – which requires specific methods, sensitivities and ethical concerns on the researchers' side. In the field of qualitative evaluation, for example, restrictions come from routines of practices (to be evaluated) and from the expectations of commissioners of the research (to have practically relevant results available after a relatively short time). These restrictions produce demands and needs different from qualitative research in the context of a dissertation project or of a funding in the context of basic research. In all these cases – from management to evaluation – specific methodological discourses have developed driven by the need to have qualitative research that is appropriate to these cases. This becomes evident in the methods that are used, in the discussions of quality of qualitative research in each field, and in ways of presenting and using results from qualitative research in each of the fields. In this third sense, it is again the proliferation and methodological refinement of qualitative research that creates a new need for taking appropriateness as a principle more seriously again and leads to a growing distinctiveness in and between the fields.

Qualitative research as an academic discipline and in applied contexts

From a more general point of view, qualitative research went through a process of establishing itself as an academic discipline. After a period of extended research, a growing number of textbooks have been published. These are general textbooks of qualitative research (such as Flick, 2006, or Silverman, 2006) or they are discipline specific (e.g. for psychology, Smith, 2003, or Bannister et al., 1994; for sociology, Denzin, 1989, etc.). Also, we can find several handbooks of qualitative research available again with a more general focus (Denzin and Lincoln, 1994, 2000, 2005b; Flick et al., 2004a; Seale et al., 2004) or with a discipline-specific focus (e.g. Willig and Stainton-Rogers, 2007, for psychology). Also, we find several journals for qualitative research in general or for qualitative research in specific areas. This comes together with attempts to formulate standards of qualitative research or at least to find more or less general answers to the question of how to judge the quality of qualitative research (see Flick, 2007, for more detail). These developments in general will lead to consolidation of qualitative research in the academic field and give an orientation for teaching, training, qualification and writing theses.

At the same time, qualitative research often is not restricted to the production of knowledge or insights for scientific purposes. Often, the intention is to change the issue under study or to produce knowledge that is practically relevant – which means relevant for producing or promoting solutions to practical problems. Approaches of participatory research or action research involve the people (or institutions) in the planning and sometimes in the doing of research who wish to produce results relevant to them (not only to scientific discourses). In such contexts, conflicts between the demands of methods and science in general and the practical purposes of research may arise. In qualitative evaluation, for example, another issue is raised. Evaluation has to produce judgements through research – does a specific program work or not? – which means researchers have to give up their neutrality at a specific point. At the same time, expectations in qualitative evaluation research are linked to sometimes rather tight time-scales; results not only have to be focused (for example on judgements and valuations), but often have to be available after a rather limited time compared to what a period for a doctoral thesis is like, for example. Routines of practice and institutional settings ask for adaptation of methodological routines and standards. In this context, a pragmatic use of methods, and the weighing of methodological standards against standards in fulfilling expectations of commissioners and against the interests of participants, often become necessary. In a methodological sense, shortcut strategies are necessary, which allow adapting methodological procedures to the conditions in the field (Flick, 2004a; Lüders, 2004a). As mentioned above, these purposes and conditions of research may lead to specific methodological problems and discourses, which again enforce the proliferation and differentiation of qualitative research in general.

Qualitative research as a moral discourse

In their definition quoted above, Denzin and Lincoln underline that the researchers' 'practices transform the world' (2005a, p. 3). Again, there are two sides of a coin to such a statement. The first is that qualitative researchers do not act as an invisible neutral in the field, but that they take part when they observe (in participant observation) or make participants reflect their life and life history (in a biographical interview), which may lead the interviewees to new insights about their situations and the world around them. The second is that qualitative research should (in general or always) engage in changing the world. Especially if we look into the third edition of Denzin and Lincoln's *Handbook of Qualitative Research* (2005b), we find many chapters spelling out what the editors set out in their preface (2005c, p. xvi): '... qualitative research is an inquiry project, but it is also a moral, allegorical, and therapeutic project'. In this reading, qualitative research is again and continuously pursuing the question that Howard Becker (1967) asked some time ago ('Whose side are we on?') and has a moral commission to take the side of the underprivileged, of minorities, or of victims of colonialization or migration. Following this understanding, qualitative research is explicitly political and intends to transform the world with its practices (to take up the quote from the definition again). However, this again is one version of defining and reading qualitative research. Beyond this understanding of qualitative research as a moral discourse, there is a more pragmatic approach to qualitative research, which sees it as an extension of the tools and potentials of social research for understanding the world and producing knowledge about it. Again, this shows the proliferation of qualitative research also at the level of basic attitudes and understandings of what research, inquiry, qualitative research, ethnography, and so on, should be about in general.

Quality and quantity: alternatives, two sides of a coin, combinations?

In the relation of qualitative and quantitative research, we again find different positions. First there is a clear rejection of the other approach on both sides of the divide. The Denzin and Lincoln handbook, for example, comes without discussing any form of combining qualitative and quantitative research. If the latter is mentioned, it is basically in contradistinction to qualitative research in order to outline the power of the first (e.g. 2005a, pp. 10–12). There are still quite a number of quantitative researchers who ignore or reject the existence of qualitative methods, of qualitative research in general and of the results produced with it. Distinction and mutual rejection is still the first way of treating both 'camps'.

However, in many areas such as evaluation research, the practice of research is characterized by a more or less pragmatic eclecticism in using a variety of qualitative and quantitative methods according to what the research question needs in order to be answered. In the context of such pragmatism, methodological reflections about how to combine qualitative and quantitative research remain rather few and limited. Combinations of qualitative and quantitative research can be viewed on different levels:

- Epistemology and methodology (including the epistemological and methodological incompatibilities of both approaches).
- Research designs, which combine or integrate qualitative and quantitative data and/or methods.
- Research methods, which are qualitative and quantitative at the same time.
- Linking the results of qualitative and quantitative research.
- Generalization.
- Assessment of research by using criteria from quantitative research to evaluate qualitative research or the other way round.

We can find several suggestions how to combine qualitative and quantitative research. Hammersley (1996, pp. 167–8) distinguishes three forms of linking qualitative and quantitative research:

- *Triangulation* of both approaches, where he sees an emphasis on the mutual assessment of results and less on the mutual extension of knowledge potentials.
- *Facilitation* highlights the supportive function of the other approach – each provides hypotheses and inspirations for pursuing analyses of the single approach.
- Both approaches can be combined as complementary research strategies.

Bryman (1992) has outlined eleven ways of integrating quantitative and qualitative research:

1 The logic of triangulation means for him to check, for example, qualitative against quantitative results.
2 Qualitative research can support quantitative research and
3 Vice versa.
4 Both are combined in or provide a more general picture of the issue under study.
5 Structural features are analysed with quantitative methods and process aspects with qualitative approaches.
6 The perspective of the researchers drives quantitative approaches, while qualitative research emphasizes the viewpoints of the subjective.
7 The problem of generality can be solved for qualitative research by adding quantitative findings.
8 Qualitative findings may facilitate the interpretation of relationships between variables in quantitative data sets.
9 The relationship between micro- and macro-levels in a substantial area can be clarified by combining qualitative and quantitative research.

10 Qualitative and quantitative research can be appropriate in different stages of the research process.

11 Hybrid forms, for example, the use of qualitative research in quasi-experimental designs (see Bryman, 1992, pp. 59–61).

In this overview we find a broad variety of alternatives. Numbers 5, 6 and 7 highlight that qualitative research can reveal different aspects compared to quantitative. Theoretical and epistemological (or moral) differences hardly play a role in Bryman's approach, which is more focused on research pragmatics. Integration of both approaches, mixed methodologies (Tashakkori and Teddlie, 2003a) and triangulation of qualitative and quantitative methods (Flick, 2007, or Kelle and Erzberger, 2004) are discussed more broadly now. Terminologies show different intentions and goals with these forms of combinations. Mixed methodology approaches are interested in pragmatic links of qualitative and quantitative research in order to end the paradigm wars of earlier times. The approach is declared to be a 'third methodological movement' (Tashakkori and Teddlie, 2003b, p. ix). Quantitative research and methods are seen as the first movement, qualitative research as the second. The goals of a methodological discussion here are to clarify the 'nomenclature', questions of design and applications of mixed methodologies research and of inferences in this context. From a methodological point of view, a paradigmatic foundation of mixed methodologies research is the aim. Using the concept of paradigms in this context, however, shows that the authors start from two closed approaches, which can be differentiated, combined or rejected, without reflecting the concrete methodological problems of combining them.

The claims for mixed methodologies research are outlined as follows: 'We proposed that a truly mixed approach methodology (a) would incorporate multiple approaches in all stages of the study (i.e., problem identification, data collection, data analysis, and final inferences) and (b) would include a transformation of the data and their analysis through another approach' (Tashakkori and Teddlie, 2003b, p. xi). The concept of integrating qualitative and quantitative approaches goes one step further, aiming at developing integrated research design and in particular at integrating qualitative and quantitative results (Kelle and Erzberger, 2004). More recent versions of triangulation, on the other hand, aim at combining the strengths of qualitative and quantitative research designs, methods of both types and results they produce by taking into account the different theoretical backgrounds (see Flick, 2006, chap. 2).

If we pick up the issue of linking qualitative and quantitative research at this point, it is not the intention to see this as the future direction of social research or as a suggestion to give up the principles and uniqueness of qualitative research. To consider ways of linking both approaches rather seems necessary for three reasons:

- First of all, there are indeed issues of research demanding both approaches to be combined.
- Secondly, pragmatic mixed methods combinations are in fashion at the moment. This is not only the case because they promise a simplification of a proliferating field – the diversities of social research. And they seem to be a way to end methodological discussions in which the appropriateness of quantitative research has been questioned.
- Thirdly, if for one of the two reasons above, combinations of qualitative and quantitative research become necessary, we should try to spell them out more explicitly at the levels of theory, methodology, research practice and interpretation of findings.

Research perspectives

Seen from a more comprehensive point of view, we can identify several research perspectives in social research. Some of them are purely quantitative oriented (which means basically that there are no qualitative research components involved). Here, we can distinguish several approaches – survey, epidemiological, standardized and experimental research, to name a few. Some of the perspectives are based on a combination of qualitative and quantitative research. As should have become clear already, we see different versions again. And finally, we can find several research perspectives that are mainly or exclusively qualitative in nature. Coming back to qualitative research, we can at least see three perspectives: a first overview is given in Table 1.1.

Theoretical points of reference in the first perspective are based on traditions of symbolic interactionism and phenomenology. A second main line is anchored theoretically in ethnomethodology and constructionism and interested in routines of everyday life and in the making of social reality. Structuralist or psychoanalytic positions, which assume unconscious psychological structures and mechanisms and latent social configurations, are the third point of reference. These three major perspectives differ in objectives of research and in the methods they employ. Authors like Lüders and Reichertz (1986) juxtapose, first, approaches highlighting the 'viewpoint of the subject' and a second group aiming at describing the processes in the production of existing (everyday, institutional or more general, social) situations, milieus and social order (e.g. in ethnomethodological analyses of language). The third approach is characterized by a (mostly hermeneutic) reconstruction of 'deep structures generating action and meaning' in the sense of psychoanalytic or objective-hermeneutic conceptions (see Flick, 2006, for more details).

The most important qualitative methods for collecting and analyzing data can be located in these research perspectives as follows. In the first perspective, semi-structured or narrative interviews and procedures of coding and content analysis are dominant. In the second research perspective, data are collected in focus

TABLE 1.1   Research perspectives in qualitative research

	Approaches to subjective viewpoints	Description of the making of social situations	Hermeneutic analysis of underlying structures
Theoretical positions	Symbolic interactionism Phenomenology	Ethnomethodology Constructionism	Psychoanalysis Genetic structuralism
Methods of data collection	Semi-structured interviews Narrative interviews	Focus groups Ethnography Participant observation Recording interactions Collecting documents	Recording interactions Photography Film
Methods of interpretation	Theoretical coding Content analysis Narrative analysis Hermeneutic methods	Conversation analysis Discourse analysis Analysis of documents	Objective hermeneutics Deep hermeneutics

groups, ethnography or (participant) observation and by recording interactions on audio- or videotape. These data are then analyzed by using discourse or conversation analyses. From the angle of the third perspective, data are mainly collected by recording interactions and by using visual material (photos or films). These then undergo one of the different versions of hermeneutic analysis (Hitzler and Eberle, 2004).

Theory and epistemology of qualitative research

As mentioned before, qualitative research is not based on a singular theoretical program, but draws on several theoretical backgrounds. However, the distinction between positivism and constructionism underlies epistemological discussion of qualitative research quite widely. According to Oakley (1999), this distinction is often linked to the context of feminism in qualitative research, too. Positivism as an epistemological program originally comes from natural sciences and therefore is used more as a negative foil from which to distinguish one's own research. But what positivism really means is seldom spelled out in social science discussions.

Bryman (2004, p. 11) summarizes several assumptions of positivism. Only knowledge of phenomena confirmed by the senses can be warranted as knowledge (phenomenalism). Theories are used to generate hypotheses that can be tested and allow explanations of laws to be assessed (deductivism). Knowledge can be produced by collecting facts that provide the basis for laws (inductivism). Science

11

must and can be conducted in a way that is value-free and thus objective. And finally, a clear distinction between scientific and normative statements is seen. Positivism often is associated with realism. Both assume that natural and social sciences should and can apply the same principles to collecting and analyzing data and that there is a world out there (an external reality) separate from our descriptions of it. However, the use of the word 'positivism' in debates about qualitative research is often criticized: Hammersley (1995, p. 2) notes, 'all one can reasonably infer from unexplicated usage of the word "positivism" in the social research literature is that the writer disapproves of whatever he or she is referring to'.

To this position, social constructionism (or constructivism) is juxtaposed (see also Flick, 2004b). A number of programs with different starting points are subsumed under these labels. What is common to all constructionist approaches is that they examine the relationship to reality by dealing with constructive processes in approaching it. Examples of constructions can be found on different levels:

- In the tradition of Piaget, cognition, perception of the world and knowledge about it are seen as constructs. Radical constructivism (Glasersfeld, 1995) takes this thought to the point where every form of cognition, because of the neurobiological process involved, has direct access only to images of the world and of reality, but not of both.
- Social constructivism in the tradition of Schütz (1962), Berger and Luckmann (1966) and Gergen (1999) inquires into the social conventionalization, perception and knowledge in everyday life.
- Constructivist sociology of science, 'laboratory-constructivist' research (Knorr-Cetina, 1981), seeks to establish how social, historical, local, pragmatic and other factors influence scientific discovery in such a way that scientific facts may be regarded as social constructs ('local products').

Constructionism is not a unified program, but is developing in parallel fashion in a number of disciplines: psychology, sociology, philosophy, neurobiology, psychiatry and information science. It informs many qualitative research programs with the approach that the realities we study are social products of the actors, of interactions and institutions.

Even if neither constructionism nor the theoretical backgrounds of qualitative research can be seen as unified approaches to the world to study, but are some kind of kaleidoscope of different accents and focuses in understanding parts of the world, we can note some basic theoretical assumptions common to the variety of qualitative research programs (see Flick et al., 2004b, p. 7). These assumptions show that people, institutions and interactions are involved in producing the realities in which they live or occur and that these productive efforts are based on processes of meaning-making. 'Objective' life circumstances (such as an illness) become relevant for the life world at least to a great extent through the subjective meanings attached to them. If we want to understand these processes of meaning-making, we should start from reconstructing how people, institutions and communications construct their worlds or social reality in our research. These assumptions are the theoretical and epistemological background for using methods such as interviews (see Kvale, 2007, and Gibbs, 2007), for understanding how individuals are engaged in that meaning-making, and thus for understanding the issues through their perspective, or to use focus groups (see Barbour, 2007), ethnography (see Angrosino, 2007), conversation analysis (Rapley, 2007) or visual methods (Banks, 2007) to show how meanings are built up in interactive processes or in objects and representations.

Qualitative research: methods and attitudes

As may have become obvious already, there is a wide range of different methods in qualitative research available now. It may even be a confusing variety of alternatives, which could be used to answer a research question. Despite all the literature available on the market of qualitative research textbooks, monographs, journal articles and book chapters, there is still some need for methodological clarification and development, which will be met by this *Kit* as a whole and by the individual books in it.

- First of all, according to the principle of appropriateness mentioned above, it still seems necessary to continue to develop new methods in qualitative research. Although there are a variety of interview methods available (see Kvale, 2007), it might still be necessary to develop new forms of interviews for new types of research questions or of participants in a study, when the existing methods are not perfectly suitable.
- Second, we need to further develop our knowledge about the existing methods, of how to use them and of what the major stepping-stones of their use are like. We need more methodological and practical reflections of the application of existing methods, of their possible refinements and of their limits.
- Third, we need clearer advice about when to use a specific method (instead of other methods available). What makes researchers decide to use a specific method, what should guide their decisions and what is the role of (methodological) habits in qualitative research?
- Qualitative research is not so much the formalized application of methodological routines as it is in the case of measurement-based research. In our realm, intuition in the field and in the contact with its members, but also in making a specific method work, plays a much bigger role. Therefore, we should know more about how intuition in research works, and more generally, how research practices and routines work in qualitative research.
- Also, there is still a need to think more about how different methods and steps in the research process fit together – in data collection and interpretation, for example.

13

- Finally, there is still a need to understand more about how qualitative researchers judge the quality of qualitative research – what makes research good research in the eyes of the researchers themselves, but also in those of the recipients of results?

Thus, there is still a need to elaborate our knowledge about the scope and the limits of specific qualitative methods and about how they are used in the day-to-day practice of qualitative research.

However, qualitative research still remains more than just using one or the other method in order to answer a research question. Qualitative research still is based on specific attitudes – of openness towards who and what is studied, of flexibility in approaching a field and moving in it, of understanding a subject's or a field's structure rather than of projecting a structure into what is studied, and so on. In developing qualitative research, in teaching it and in applying it, we should try to keep the balance between technical skills and the attitude that is appropriate to qualitative research.

Structure of the book and of *The SAGE Qualitative Research Kit*

Plan of the book

In this book, we will unfold these introductory remarks about qualitative research and develop a brief overview of qualitative research and the research process from the angle of designing qualitative research. The next chapter is about how to develop a research question from a general idea or interest. Chapter 3 will address basic strategies of sampling in qualitative research and how to find access to a field. Chapter 4 will unfold the concept of research design in qualitative research in more detail, focusing on influences and components in research designs and discussing basic designs and examples. Chapter 5 will inform you about necessary resources and stepping-stones you might be confronted with in the field. In Chapter 6 we will address the quality of qualitative research from the perspective of research design and continue this discussion for research ethics in Chapter 7. The remaining chapters (8–10) will give you a brief overview of the most important methods in qualitative research. Chapter 8 will address methods for collecting verbal data in interviews and focus groups, Chapter 9 is about ethnography and visual methods, and Chapter 10 will inform about basic analytic strategies in qualitative research. The focus of all three chapters is again designing qualitative research. The final chapter will draw some conclusions, discuss the relation of research design and proposal writing from two sides, and give an outlook to the other books in *The SAGE Qualitative Research Kit*.

The books in The SAGE Qualitative Research Kit

While in this book the framework of qualitative research is outlined and methods are basically addressed from a specific viewpoint (designing qualitative research), the other books in *The SAGE Qualitative Research Kit* are much more detailed in presenting methodological approaches. Kvale (2007) will give an introduction to using interviews. Barbour (2007) will do the same for using focus groups. Angrosino (2007) discusses ethnography and participant observation, whereas Banks (2007) unfolds the use of visual data (photos, film, video) in qualitative research. Gibbs (2007) introduces approaches of coding and categorizing in analyzing qualitative data and pays some extra attention to using computers and software in this context. Rapley (2007) presents approaches for studying conversations, discourses and documents. In the last book (Flick, 2007), the issue of quality in qualitative research will be discussed in more detail.

Key points

- Qualitative research is in a process of proliferation into different research perspectives and fields of application.
- Nevertheless, there are common features and issues in this variety.
- Appropriateness can be seen as a guiding principle across this variety.
- Qualitative research is located between using methods and taking an attitude.

Further reading

Besides the other books of this *Kit*, which go much more into detail of the issues that were mentioned briefly in this introduction, four books are suggested as further reading, addressing the different areas mentioned here from different angles:

Denzin, N. and Lincoln, Y.S. (eds) (2005b) *The Sage Handbook of Qualitative Research* (3rd ed.). London: Sage.
Flick, U. (2006) *An Introduction to Qualitative Research* (3rd ed.). London: Sage.
Flick, U., Kardorff, E. von and Steinke, I. (eds) (2004a) *A Companion to Qualitative Research*. London: Sage.
Seale, C., Gobo, G., Gubrium, J. and Silverman, D. (2004) (eds) *Qualitative Research Practice*. London: Sage.

2
From an idea to a research question

Chapter objectives
After reading this chapter, you should

- see how personal or scientific interests and experiences are the background to developing a research interest in many cases;
- know more about the process from such an interest to a research question; and
- see the relevance of taking a perspective and of using theory in qualitative research.

In this chapter, we will change the focus from more general considerations about qualitative research. Here, we will address issues of planning and preparing a study as a preliminary to the actual research acts in the field. For this purpose, we will discuss general issues and problems of planning by using concrete examples of my own research. Very generally speaking, these projects focus on professionals' concepts of health and ageing (Flick et al., 2002, 2003) and on homeless adolescents' health (Flick and Röhnsch, 2007).

Interest and ideas for research: examples

In the history of qualitative research, we find several examples of how ideas for research came up and developed into research questions. For example, Glaser and Strauss (1965) developed the idea of studying 'awareness of dying' after they had had special experiences when their mothers died in hospitals. The authors (pp. 286–7) describe in some detail how these experiences turned their own interest and awareness to processes in communicating with and about dying persons, which they later described as awareness contexts. In this example, the background for developing a research idea, interest and question was a personal one – the recent personal experiences of the researchers.

Hochschild (1983, p. ix) describes early experiences as a child in her family's home and social life as the source and starting point for her later 'interest in how people manage emotions'. Her parents, being part of the US Foreign Service, gave her the chance to see – and interpret – the different forms of smiles (and their meanings) produced by diplomats from different cultural backgrounds. Hochschild learned from these experiences that emotional expressions like smiles and handshakes conveyed messages on several levels – from person to person as well as from the country the person represented as an emissary to the country the other person represented. This led to the specific research interest (much later of course):

> I wanted to discover what it is that we act upon. And so I decided to explore the idea that emotion functions as a messenger from the self, an agent that gives us an instant report on the connection between what we are seeing and what we had expected to see and tells us what we feel ready to do about it. (1983, p. x)

From that interest she developed a study (*The Managed Heart*) of two sorts of public-contact workers (flight attendants and bill collectors) in order to show how emotion work functions to induce or suppress emotions when doing their jobs in contact with their clients.

Marie Jahoda (1995; see also Fleck, 2004, p. 59) describes how the impulse for her study with Paul Lazarsfeld and Hans Zeisel on *Marienthal: The Sociology of an Unemployed Community* (Jahoda et al., 1933/1971) came from the Austrian Marxist theoretician Otto Bauer, leader of the Social Democrat party in Austria. Backgrounds were the Great Depression of 1929 and also the political interest and orientation of the researchers, which made them pick up the idea of studying how a community changes when the majority of its members become unemployed. From this general impulse, they developed as a research question what the attitude of the population towards unemployment and what the social consequences of unemployment were like.

If we compare these examples, they show the different sources for developing research interests, ideas and subsequently research questions. They range from very personal experiences (Glaser and Strauss) to social experiences and circumstances (Hochschild) and societal problems and political commissioning (Jahoda et al.). In each case, a general curiosity arose, which then was pursued

17

and put into concrete terms. Of course, there are other sources for research interests, which are located more inside the scientific system than in our examples. A lot of research results from previous research, questions that remained unanswered, new questions resulting from previous findings and the like. Sometimes researchers have a special methodological interest, which makes them look for a good case to explore a method's potential or limits.

In the case of our own study on professionals' health concepts, the backgrounds of our research interest had two sources. First, the research team shared a longer engagement in the development of public health (see Schwartz, 2003) and new public health (Flick, 2002) as a perspective for research and for professional training and, second, an interest in subjective understandings of health (see Flick 1998a, 1998b). From this, we developed an interest in how the ideas of health, health promotion and prevention (as some of the core concepts of public health) had an impact on the day-to-day practices in health institutions. In this example, the idea for research was rooted in a scientific interest as well as in a political concern (how to use public health concepts for transforming and improving the existing health system).

Taking a research perspective

For developing a research project from such an idea and for elaborating a research question from it, the second step (after having such an idea) is to take a research perspective. In the case of Glaser and Strauss, this perspective was to develop a theory for an area in which theoretical knowledge or explanations were missing. For this purpose, they collected and analysed all sorts of data by comparing and systematizing the bits and pieces of observation they made. The aim of their research was to identify a basic – core – concept, which allowed them to relate, systematize and understand these bits and pieces and to explain how the social phenomenon worked which they were interested in. Thus, their research perspective was focused on theory development, on reducing variety – by finding one core concept – and finding structure – in their case four forms of the core concept. For explaining how communication about death and dying in the hospital worked, why people often did not talk about the situation and near death of a patient, Glaser and Strauss (1965) developed a theory, which was organized around the core concept of 'awareness context' and four versions of it. The research perspective they took was to develop theory from data, which has since become one of the basic perspectives in qualitative research.

A second perspective, which can be taken to analyse social processes, is to focus on personal experiences of people who have had certain experiences. Such a biographical perspective can start from a specific event and analyze examples of living with the consequences of these events or of dealing with it in general. The event can be a personal one – like the beginning or diagnosis of a chronic or terminal illness (see Frank, 1995) – or a more general one like a political change. For understanding how people concerned with this event experience it, deal with it, arrange themselves with the consequences and perhaps reorganize their lives for coping with the event, a biographical perspective is taken in research. This perspective aims at giving individuals with this experience the space to recount their lives in an interview. The analysis then focuses on comparing these experiences for developing, for example, a typology of the different ways of living with this experience. The next step then can again be to develop a theory of coping with the event under study, but this step is not necessarily taken in every study (see Rosenthal and Fischer-Rosenthal, 2004).

In our own research project on professionals' health concepts, we started from a theoretical perspective in order to follow how this was transferred into everyday knowledge in professional practice. Here, we were not so much interested in finding a central concept or in developing a theory. Thus, our interest was not so much to reduce the variety in the data to one core concept or theoretical model. Rather we were interested to see how the theoretical knowledge under study – concepts from new public health – were adopted by professional groups, and how they differ in this sort of adoption. Therefore we took up social representations (see Moscovici, 1973, 1998; Flick, 1998a; Flick and Foster, 2007, for more details) as a theoretical perspective for our study. A social representation traditionally is understood as

> a system of values, ideas and practices with a twofold function; first to establish an order which will enable individuals to orientate themselves in their material and social world and to master it; and secondly to enable communication to take place among the members of a community by providing them with a code for social exchange and a code for naming and classifying unambiguously the various aspects of their world and their individual and group history. (Moscovici, 1973, p. xvii)

Our interest was in how far two professional groups used concepts, approaches and goals coming from new public health in their day-to-day practice. Social representation theory describes how concepts and ideas from a scientific theory are taken up in everyday life, how these are objectified and anchored in routines and practices (see Fig. 2–1).

These three examples show how different research perspectives can be taken in qualitative research for studies in very similar areas. Grounded theory research is an example of a bottom-up perspective (from phenomena and practices to theory and explanation). Social representation theory is an example of a top-down perspective (from theoretical concepts and scientific models to everyday practices). Biographical research is an example of a perspective starting from a mid-level

FIGURE 2.1 Social representations of health and illness

(events and coping strategies). It could go either way: to develop a theory from analyzing biographical experiences and accounts or to look into which kinds of knowledge people use for coping with an event and how they differ in this utilization.
Other ones could complement these three examples. An ethnomethodological
research perspective would be interested in analyzing everyday routines of talk and
action from a more formal perspective. Ethnography would be more interested in
close descriptions of such practices without such a formal perspective.

The important thing at this point is that qualitative researchers also need to take
a research perspective in approaching their issues and that there is more than one
research perspective available and frequently used in qualitative research.
Researchers not only need to decide on one perspective for their research but also
to choose it from the range of available alternatives. Our examples here should
show how research perspectives are chosen in approaching an issue and for formulating a research question in the widest sense (see below).

Using theory in qualitative research

That qualitative research does not build on existing theory has been a myth, which was produced by some writings of Glaser and Strauss (1967). That myth and these formulations have been revised a long time ago, for several reasons. One reason is that areas that have not been studied empirically or subject to theoretical analysis are more and more difficult to find compared to the period when Glaser and Strauss set up their research program of developing grounded theories. A second reason is that 'theory' has become much more differentiated since then – there are a lot of middle-range or even small-range theories (sometimes resulting from qualitative research) available. Also in qualitative research we have to build on existing theories and results from empirical research, unless we want to risk being naïve when starting our research.

Following what was said before, we have different sorts of theories that we are confronted with while planning a research project.

First, there are background theories that inform our research, beginning with the epistemological fundamentals of our research (for example, do we build on some sort of constructivism or on some sort of realist epistemology?)

Second, the theoretical perspective of our research program informs how we plan our concrete research. If we take a biographical perspective, this comes with a lot of assumptions about biography, about the individual as narrator, about human ability to reflect about what is happening to the individual, and so on. If we take the perspective of social representations, we assume that people (lay people and professionals) are informed by scientific or public discourses, process the knowledge coming from them in a specific way, and that social contexts influence how they do that. For example, it is implied that doctors anchor new developments in relevant sciences in their practice differently from how nurses do. These assumptions are not yet specific for the substantial issue of the current project but are essential for the research perspective taken.

Third, they are complemented by theoretical knowledge about the issue of research – for example, what it generally means for patients to be confronted with a terminal illness or that health promotion goes beyond or starts earlier than curing existing diseases. This theoretical knowledge comes from the literature and the existing body of research.

Fourth, we use theoretical assumptions linked to the concrete methods we use in the project – a narrative interview comes along with assumptions about what happens when people talk about a crucial experience in the form of a life story and so on.

Thus, we have four forms of theoretical knowledge coming from epistemology, from the research perspective, from the issue of research and from the methods we intend to use. All these forms of knowledge play an implicit or (better) explicit role in how we do our research and before that, how we plan it.

Developing a research question

Before we can address an issue empirically, we should clarify for ourselves (and for later readers) what it is exactly that we want to study. A research interest and a research perspective are necessary steps. In most cases, however, both are not focused enough for developing a research instrument (like an interview guide) or a research design (whom to interview) or for having a clear and relevant set of data in the end (see Flick, 2006, chap. 9 for details). Experience from my own research and even more from supervising and consulting other people in their research has shown how decisive it is for the success of a project to have a clear and explicitly formulated research question. It decides about what is important (to collect as data, to analyse in it, etc.) and even more about what is less important and should be left out (for the current project). However, there are different ways leading to such a research question: One way is to start with defining and formulating your research and then to pursue it through your empirical work in order to find an answer to it. The other way is to start with a general observation and to make the research question more focused under way, as in the case of Glaser and Strauss's study (1965) on dying and death in the hospital. In the conceptualization of grounded theory, the term 'research question' does not play a major role (1967; see also Charmaz, 2006). However, for beginners in qualitative or grounded theory research, it seems more than helpful to have a clear research question to answer with their research as a guideline. Finally, even when we start with a more or less general research question, it will be refined and reformulated, sometimes refocused in the course of the project (see Flick, 2006, chap. 9, for more details).

In a biographical research project, the formulation of a research question includes the event that the project is referring to, the idea of a group of persons or a specific context of experiencing this event, and a period in the life history, which will be focused in the empirical approach. In the case of illness experiences, it is often the time since the outbreak or diagnosis of the illness, but frequently the focus is also on the period before that event.

In our project on professionals' health concepts mentioned above (Flick et al., 2002), we were interested generally in whether and how far a public health orientation had arrived at some of the key institutions of home-care services in the health field. This is of course not yet a research question that you can use for starting an empirical study. So we had to develop this general interest into a more focused perspective. Therefore, we first focused on health concepts held by home-care nurses and general practitioners. Then we focused on the attitude towards prevention and health promotion as parts of their work and more concretely with a special part of their clientele – the elderly. Against this background, we developed a set of questions we wanted to pursue in a study using interviews:

- What are the concepts of health held by doctors and nurses?
- Which dimensions of health representations are relevant for professional work with the elderly?
- What is the attitude of professionals towards prevention and health promotion for the elderly?
- What are the concepts of ageing held by general practitioners and home-care nurses? What is the relation of these concepts with those of health?
- What relevance do professionals ascribe to their own concepts of health for their own professional practice?
- Are there any relations between the concepts of health and professional training and experience?

We took these research questions as a starting point for developing an instrument for episodic interviews (see Flick 2006, 2007) with doctors and nurses. Looking back on this project, we thought critically about the number of different research questions included in the above list. Especially for novices to qualitative research, it is suggested to concentrate on one or two such questions in planning a similar project to the one we did.

Conclusion

These steps in planning and preparing a study are important to make a design and a study work in the concrete case. The times when we could 'just do it' (as Glaser, 1992, still or again suggests) are over for qualitative research as well. Researchers who start a study using qualitative methods today for addressing a problem they are interested in, are confronted with enormous background knowledge they could use for making their research more successful. Therefore, it seems necessary to clarify the research question and to get acquainted with the existing literature about the research. You should also carefully plan and decide for a research perspective and do your homework in the planning phase of your project. This includes preparing your access to the field, clarifying your relations to the field and the members and institutions in it, and becoming an expert in the methods you and your research team want to use.

≡≡≡ Key points

For preparing and planning a qualitative study that is up-to-date, it seems necessary:

- to develop a general idea and interest into a more or less focused research question;
- to take a research perspective (and to know why); and
- to get updated with theory and literature on several levels (epistemological, theoretical, methodical, about the issue itself, etc.)

Further reading

In these texts, the examples used here for clarifying the relation of ideas, research perspectives and research questions are unfolded in a little more detail:

Charmaz, K. (2006) *Constructing Grounded Theory – A Practical Guide Through Qualitative Analysis*. Thousand Oaks, CA: Sage.

Fleck, C. (2004) 'Marie Jahoda', in U. Flick, E. von Kardorff and I. Steinke (eds), *A Companion to Qualitative Research*. London: Sage, pp. 58–62.

Flick, U. (2006) *An Introduction to Qualitative Research* (3rd ed.), Part 7. London: Sage.

Flick, U. and Foster, J. (2007). 'Social representations', in C. Willig, and W. Stainton-Rogers (eds), *The Sage Handbook of Qualitative Research in Psychology*. London: Sage (in press).

3
Sampling, selecting and access

Chapter objectives
After reading this chapter, you should

- see the different logics of sampling in qualitative research;
- know about the levels on which sampling decisions are taken in qualitative research;
- understand that sampling of cases is complemented by sampling in cases;
- know more about finding access to a field.

Sometimes it is doubted whether sampling is the right term if you do qualitative research (e.g. Maxwell, 2005, p. 88). But in qualitative research, we of course face the problem addressed with this term as well: we have to select the 'right' cases, groups and materials in a somehow defined way – so that we can do our study with limited resources – from a more or less infinite horizon of possible selections. And with what we select, we want to make statements that we can generalize in one way or the other – in most cases at least beyond the research situations and beyond the four or forty people we interviewed, for example. As this problem is similar in qualitative research to other forms of social research in a very general way, I will continue to use the term 'sampling' here.

Logics of sampling in qualitative research

In quantitative research, sampling normally is formalized – for example, drawing a random sample from a population, having some quotas in the sample and the like. The idea here is to represent a larger population in its features and their distribution in the sample that has been drawn from it. Samples here should be representative in order to allow referring the findings from studying the sample to (larger) populations. Thus, sampling here pursues the logic of (statistical) generalization.

Sampling in qualitative research can follow different logics. We can distinguish a more formalized sampling from more purposive and flexible ways of doing it. In the first alternative, for example, the number of cases (e.g. interviewees) is defined in advance including a distribution over certain features. We might define at the beginning of our empirical work how many female and male participants we need to interview, set up a range of years for their age, define other criteria like specific professions and the like. The idea in the background is that demographic features (such as gender, age and profession) are helpful for accessing the variety in what we study and that we should orient on these features to include this variety in our sample. If we study health concepts, for example, we might start from the assumption that these concepts are different for men and women and are changing when people grow older and therefore define a sample of men and women of different ages. Implicitly or explicitly, we define groups for later comparison with such a sample – that we systematically will look for differences among older and younger people while analyzing the data.

A different logic is to define the cases in our study more purposively and step by step. In grounded theory research, sampling decisions are taken neither formally nor in advance, but during the progress of the research on the background of collecting and analyzing the data continuously. While in more formal forms of sampling, ideas about what should be in the sample and how to find it are behind the logic of sampling, in theoretical sampling it is more the idea of what is still missing in the data (and the insights they make possible) which drives sampling decisions (see Charmaz, 2006, for theoretical sampling in more detail and Flick, 2007, chap. 4).

For sampling, a distinction that Miles and Huberman (1994, pp. 16–18) made for research designs becomes relevant. They distinguish tight from loose research designs and see advantages for both depending on the concrete project and its circumstances. A tight research design is characterized by narrow and restricted questions and also by prestructured selection procedures. The degree of openness in the field of investigation and the empirical material remains rather limited. Miles and Huberman suggest such a design for researchers who lack experience with qualitative research. They are also helpful when the research is based on clearly defined constructs, and when it is restricted to the investigation of particular relationships in familiar contexts. In such cases, they see loose designs as a detour to the expected results. Tighter designs make it easier to decide which data or extracts from the data are relevant for the investigation and what is not relevant. They also make it easier, for example, to compare and summarize data from different interviews or observations. They will be based on a clearly defined plan for sampling, for example.

Loose designs on the other hand are characterized by less defined concepts and operate, in the beginning, with hardly fixed methodological procedures. For Miles and Huberman, this type of design is appropriate for researchers who are experienced with qualitative research in different fields, when new fields are studied and the theoretical constructs and concepts are not very developed. Loose designs are more informed by the methodological suggestions of Glaser and Strauss (1967), for example in their handling of theoretical sampling with great openness and flexibility (see also Flick, 2007, chap. 4).

This distinction of designs is a context for the alternatives for sampling – more formal and more purposeful variants – mentioned above. Formal ways of sampling are part of a more or less tight design and easier to handle for less experienced researchers. Purposive sampling comes with a need for more openness and flexibility and thus is more likely to be a part of a loose design and is easier to manage, if the researchers are more experienced.

Suggestions for sampling

Sampling not only focuses the selection of people to be interviewed for example, or situations to be observed, but also the selection of sites in which such persons or situations can be expected to be found. Sampling in qualitative research in most cases is not oriented on a formal (e.g. random) selection of a part of an existing or assumed population. Rather it is conceived as a way of setting up a collection of deliberately selected cases, materials or events for constructing a corpus of empirical examples for studying the phenomenon of interest in the most instructive way. Therefore, most suggestions for qualitative sampling are around a concept of purpose. Taking sampling in qualitative research seriously is a way of managing diversity (see Flick, 2007, chap. 4) so that the variation and variety in the phenomenon under study can be captured in the empirical material as far as possible.

Patton (2002) suggests the following alternatives of purposive sampling:

- First you may try to integrate purposively *extreme* or deviant cases. If you study processes of coping with a chronic illness, you might look for those cases that are most successful in integrating their illness in their everyday life and for those who have the biggest problems in adapting to the illness in their day-to-day practice and compare both. Here, the field under study is disclosed from its extremities to arrive at an understanding of the field as a whole.

- An alternative is to look for the particularly *typical* cases, i.e. those cases in which success and failure are particularly typical for the average or the majority of the cases. Here, the field is disclosed from inside and from its centre.
- The third of Patton's suggestions aims at the *maximal variation* in the sample. This means that you try to integrate only a few cases, but those that are as different as possible, to disclose the range of variation and differentiation in the field.
- You may also select cases according to the *intensity* with which the interesting features, processes, experiences, etc., are given or assumed in them. Either you look for those cases with the greatest intensity or systematically integrate and compare cases with different intensities.
- To select critical cases, aim at those cases in which the experiences or processes to be studied become especially clear – for example in the opinion of experts in the field.
- It may be instructive to select *sensitive cases* in order to illustrate positive findings of a study most effectively – which is an argument for integrating them. However, where these cases might be problematic from an ethical point of view, you should rather exclude them.
- In his list of alternatives, Patton mentions the criterion of *convenience,* which refers to the selection of those cases that are the easiest to access under given conditions. However, this is not really a suggestion for how to plan a sampling but rather a second-best choice, if none of the more defined alternatives can be applied. Although this strategy may reduce the effort, it should only be chosen if it is the only way to do a study because of limited resources of time and people or due to problems of applying a more directed way of sampling.

Miles and Huberman (1994, p. 28) add several other forms of sampling for qualitative research, which are more or less systematic and more or less pragmatic. They mention the use of a *homogeneous sample* in particular for group interviewing or of a *theory-based sample* derived from a specific theoretical construct, which is to be elaborated empirically. They also suggest mixed forms like a *random purposeful sampling* (when a consistently purposeful sampling would produce too large numbers of cases to be handled) or *stratified purposeful sampling* (based on building subgroups in the sample for comparison) or *mixed sampling* (putting multiple interests and needs into concrete terms in one sample). Finally they list *snowball sampling* (going from one case to the next, asking interviewees for other people who might be relevant for the study and the like).

Sampling decisions can pursue different goals – sometimes in the same study. One is to find the most typical or the most developed case(s) for studying in the phenomenon under study. Therefore we often look for people with a long experience with the issue we want to interview them about or those who are really in the position to apply the professional practice we are interested in. In contrast to traditional psychology, where student populations are the empirical basis for most of the studies, qualitative researchers are interested in people who are 'really' concerned and experienced with the issue under study. So we are looking for the core cases for the experience, knowledge, practice, etc., we want to study. In this way, our sample should be representative – not in a statistical way or in representing the reality in a basic population. Rather, our cases should be able to represent the relevance of the phenomenon we want to study in our research participants' experience and concern with this phenomenon. In most studies, we are interested in the variety of experiences and concerns, so that we should not only have comparably central or core cases, but also the variance in the field and the differences in the links to the issue. This calls for looking for cases at the edge of the field under study, extreme cases, cases with different intensity, etc. These different goals are perhaps difficult to take into account at the same time – for example, when a sample structure is defined at the beginning of a research project and then just applied. It is much easier to follow these different goals one after the other, when we take our sampling decisions step by step – first look for the 'core' cases and then for the variation in the field. That is one reason why sampling strategies in qualitative research are often strategies of gradual selection (see Flick, 2006, chap. 11) – most prominently in the case of theoretical sampling in grounded theory research. However, in recent publications, theoretical sampling is more clearly distinguished from other forms of sampling, such as initial sampling or sampling oriented on population distributions or negative cases (Charmaz, 2006, p. 100). As Maxwell (2005, pp. 89–90) underlines, sampling should be oriented towards collecting the heterogeneity in the field and towards allowing as much comparison as possible. If the cases in our sample are too similar, it will be difficult to make meaningful comparison among them; if they are too heterogeneous, it will be difficult to identify common features in them.

Depending on the research question, the aims of the study and also the methods to be used, sampling can refer to several levels. A first distinction here is between person- and situation-oriented sampling. A second distinction refers to sampling of cases and sampling within cases. A third distinction is between sampling *of* materials and sampling *in* materials.

Sampling people

Qualitative research is often focused on persons or groups of persons. Interviewing people for their experiences with chronic illness means that you have to look for people who have made these experiences and you will be looking for a number of people who have made it in different intensity, for a longer or shorter time or with different types of chronic illnesses, etc. If you are interested in expert knowledge about institutional decision-making, you have to define what you consider as expertise in this context, reflect about who might have this expertise and in which position in the institution such expertise may be located. Then you will select actors from these different positions, maybe from different hierarchies in the institution, for doing an expert interview with them. In this case a specific professional position or function is the criterion in the background of your sampling decision.

When you do an interview study of the kind just mentioned (see also Kvale, 2007), it may sometimes be difficult to know in advance or at the beginning who will be the right persons to address your questions. In most cases you will be interested in finding the most knowledgeable people for giving you information about your topic and you will be looking for different points of view.

The term 'sampling' often is associated with selecting the 'right' cases from a known reservoir of cases and that this can be done at one time. In the research practice of qualitative research with interviews also, it is often an iterative process. When you orient yourself in the field of your study, you develop more and more knowledge about this field and the people in it. Therefore your procedure in sampling and selecting people might change along the way, the more you find out about who might be most knowledgeable and who might have a different point of view compared to other or average members of your field.

Selecting sites and events

If you are interested in how people communicate about the issue of your research in specific contexts, for example adolescents with chronic illness in their peer group, you will need to sample situations in which such a communication takes place. If you are interested in observing specific practices, you need to find and sample settings in which you can expect these practices to happen. Especially if you are interested in practices in institutional contexts, you have to find and choose settings inside these institutions, in which you can access the practices you want to study. For example, if you are interested in studying decision-making about pupils' school performances and career, you have to take sampling decisions on different levels. First you will draw a sample of schools (or school types), which you expect to cover the range of variation for your issue. Then you will need to identify those situations in which the actors in the field talk about the issue of school performance, exchange information for preparing decisions and make the decisions. If there is a formal framework for this – for example, a regular meeting among the teachers once a month or at the end of the school term – then you should take a sample of such meetings in one or more schools. If these decisions are more or less prepared or taken outside such a formal setting, you have to identify those situations in which the relevant steps are taken and try to integrate these situations into your sampling. Maybe you have to go to classroom situations to analyze the negotiations of teacher and pupil at the occasion of classroom performances of pupils for understanding the way decisions are prepared and taken.

This means, in such an example, that your sampling process will consist of several steps. You will select a site (or a type of site) – in our case the school or several schools. Then you will identify situations in this site that are relevant for your issue – in our case, teachers' meetings. Then again you will try to select those concrete situations in which your issue will become visible – in our case those meetings concerned with decisions about grading of pupils. And finally, you will identify other types of situations by which your issue is influenced as well – in our case classroom situations, etc. Again, your knowledge about the 'right' situations and about the 'right' variety of such situations will develop along the progress of your research, so that the classical notion of sampling – selecting examples from a given set of cases or population – will unlikely be fit to describe the process.

The selection of sites and situations is most relevant for ethnographic research, for using participant observation (Angrosino, 2007) and for studies of communication such as in conversation analysis (Rapley, 2007).

Constructing groups

Sampling in qualitative research can also take a third point of reference beyond persons and situations. In focus groups (see Barbour, 2007), it is often the group that is seen as the case and not the individual participants. To find the right cases, then, means to have groups that include people with a specific relation to what is studied and with the right mixture of people, opinions and attitudes. To include the appropriate variety, then, means to have groups that are different enough to cover a range of experiences with or attitudes towards the issue. Comparison can be on the level of the different groups, the contents of their discussion and how this discussion went on. For making such a comparison most fruitful, an appropriate construction of groups in the step of sampling is essential.

The construction of groups, however, can result from sampling and selecting for an interview study that addresses individuals as well. As mentioned above, selecting people for certain features like gender, age or profession sets up groups in the study that can be a first approach for comparison – between people of a certain age, between male and female, or between professions. Such a sampling leads to the construction of groups in the study and the single participant is seen – also – as a member of a specific group (the young or the old, etc.). Again, this rationale for sampling can be a starting point and perhaps be changed in the course of the project – for example when you find out that it is not gender that makes up the difference in the experience of the chronic illness you study, but social support. In such a case, your comparison should increasingly concentrate on, for example, building a typology of support experiences in chronic illness rather than on gender issues. Selecting and comparing in research always builds on implicitly or explicitly constructing groups – even in saying this, a particular case is compared to the rest of the cases. Here we have the group of the rest of the cases as one side, and the singular or different case as a second group.

Finally, we construct groups in sampling, if we do observation and ethnography (see Angrosino, 2007) and identify a social group as relevant for our issue. For example, in our study on chronic illness of homeless adolescents in a German city, we selected a specific spot in that city where adolescents hang out who have no regular place to live. In selecting the people at this spot in a specific age group (14–25 years for being adolescents) who have a chronic illness (one of quite a variety of illnesses in this group), we construct a group out of individuals rather seeing themselves as independent of the rest of the other people in this group or of most of them. In identifying the ensemble of these people for observing them as a particular community or culture, we construct a group out of people who do not necessarily experience themselves or the other individuals in our study as members of the same group.

Constructing a corpus

If we go beyond asking or observing people or groups of people in qualitative research, the logic of sampling may change as well. When we address documents as data in research – either texts (Rapley, 2007) or images (Banks, 2007) – we often set up a collection of such documents – an archive or a corpus of materials. In such a case, we do not make a selection of persons or situations in order to produce data by applying methods to study them, but we take existing materials, which we select in order to analyze them. Thus, the sequence is turned around – first the material, then the selection, then the use of methods instead of first the selection, then the methods, and then the materials, and the methods again. This corpus can be a set of videotapes of doctor–patient interaction originally recorded for use in supervision or a number of patient files from a hospital produced for routine documentation, etc. Sampling here is strongly based on discovering the right exemplars of these documents for answering the research question. Again, this corpus can be set up at one point at the beginning of the analysis and can be redesigned during the progress of the analysis and according to the gaps in the material or analysis so far.

Sampling inside cases and materials

Sampling in qualitative research can mean different things: to select people, groups, sites and situations for collecting data or to build a corpus to set up data for an analysis. In each of these versions, sampling cases or materials is only the first step.

The sampling process continues, as you will sample statements from the host of answers or from a long life history in your interviews, which address the issue of your study directly or are relevant to it. In documents, you have to sample the passages relevant for answering your research questions or for being able to compare different documents at all. Thus, sampling in qualitative research does not only mean sampling *of* cases and materials but also sampling *inside* materials and cases. Sometimes you have to select specific cases or examples from your sample (of interviewees, for example) for working with them in more detail. In an application for funding, we once set up a hypothetical sample of interviewees that we planned to select, interview and analyze. The reviewers and the funding agency suggested selecting and interviewing twice as many participants as we intended and then taking the most promising cases into transcription and analysis. This meant we had to take a second sampling decision in the material we disposed of after interviewing.

However, sampling continues when you plan to present your findings in your report or in an article. Again you will draw a sample of the most illustrative, convincing, confirming and sometimes disputing examples from your research, as space in your medium of publication and reading capacities of your audience are limited (see also Flick, 2006, chap. 11).

All in all, sampling is a crucial step in designing qualitative research as it is the step in which you reduce the potentially infinite horizon of possible materials and cases for your study to a manageable and at the same time justifiable selection of cases and materials. You should avoid convenience sampling, and you should refrain from ways of sampling and selecting that are neither purposive nor formal. At the same time, authors such as Rubin and Rubin (1995) suggest that sampling in qualitative research should be iterative and flexible. This means you should be ready to adapt to the conditions in the field and to new insights resulting from data collection, which might suggest changes in the original sampling plan.

However, constructing a sample plan is always theoretically informed (Denzin, 1989, p. 73) and it is sometimes a theoretical effort driven by your intentions and theoretical interests. Your relation to the field, your access to the people, situations or materials will determine whether you can include what your sampling demands in the ideal case.

Examples of constructing a sample will be given at the end of Chapter 4, where examples of research designs will be outlined, including the sampling decisions taken in constructing them.

Clarifying access and necessary approval

In the period of planning your study, it is important to find access to the field in which you want to work empirically. In some cases the most important step here is to identify a field in which the experiences are made that you want to study or in which the people you want to access can be met. In our project about health concepts of homeless adolescents in Germany (Flick and Röhnsch, 2007), for example, it was a major step to find out where people living under these circumstances can be met, where they hang out, meet peers or turn to institutional help. Then the most crucial step was to be accepted by the adolescents as someone to talk to or to let take part in everyday life in the street – thus making interviews and observations possible.

In other studies working in institutions, it is often necessary and time-consuming to find out who has to agree to your study and decide about letting you in for doing your empirical work. In schools or hospitals, there are often several institutional levels to be involved before you are allowed to approach interviewees, for example. It should also be clarified which formal approval of your research has to be obtained and by whom. If institutional review boards or ethic committees have to be involved (see Chapter 7), this is a sometimes complicated process that should be started early enough and sometimes requires methodological and theoretical clarifications and commitments that are difficult to make in the early stage of a project. Finally, you should reflect which sort of formalization you plan for your relation to study participants. Is it necessary, possible and advisable to make an interview contract regulating technical details of anonymity and data protection? Is this form of informed consent about the participation in the research something you can ask from your participants in a formal way? If not, who else can give you that consent, etc. (see Flick, 2006, chap. 4 for details)?

Finding access to fields, institutions or people can be a difficult and long process. Wolff (2004) describes problems and strategies you might meet in the field, which will make your access more complicated or are used for keeping you and research in general out of an institution, for example. This analysis shows that finding access is not just a step at the beginning of your field contact or something that can be formalized by preparing an information flyer about your project. It is rather a negotiation running through several steps, facing immune reactions by the field (trying to send the 'invading' research back), based on personal trust between the field and the researcher, finding gatekeepers who open the doors to the field and to the right persons, and being clear to the field of what you expect from it.

In this context, it is important to set up a basis of informed consent – that everybody knows they are part of an ongoing research and has the right and chance to say no to any form of personal participation – in the field and with your possible participants (see Chapter 7).

Both issues of this chapter are parts of the more general topic of building a research design for a qualitative study. Sampling is a major step in constructing the research design (see also Chapter 4), finding access determines how far the plan of research formulated in this design is going to work in the concrete research practice.

====== Key points

- Sampling in qualitative research often follows a different logic than in standardized research.
- It should be oriented on some rationale according to which cases and materials are selected.
- Sampling can address different levels (sites, people, events, etc.) depending on your research question and the method you will apply.
- Sampling refers not only to selecting cases and materials but also to taking samples inside cases and materials (e.g. certain statements or parts).
- To clarify and find access to fields and people has to be carefully planned and can be a difficult process sometimes.

Further reading

In these works, issues of sampling are outlined in more detail in relation to specific methods or in general. Wolff summarizes problems of access and discusses possible solutions.

Angrosino, M. (2007) *Doing Ethnographic and Observational Research* (Book 3 of *The SAGE Qualitative Research Kit*). London: Sage.

Barbour, R. (2007) *Doing Focus Groups* (Book 4 of *The SAGE Qualitative Research Kit*). London: Sage.

Kvale, S. (2007) *Doing Interviews* (Book 2 of *The SAGE Qualitative Research Kit*) London: Sage.

Merkens, H. (2004) 'Selection procedures, sampling, case construction', in U. Flick, E. von Kardorff and I. Steinke (eds), *A Companion to Qualitative Research*. London, Sage, pp. 165–71.

Rapley, T. (2007) *Doing Conversation, Discourse and Document Analysis* (Book 7 of *The SAGE Qualitative Research Kit*) London: Sage.

Rubin, H.J. and, Rubin, I.S. (1995) *Qualitative Interviewing*. Thousand Oaks, CA: Sage (2nd ed. 2005).

Wolff, S. (2004) 'Ways into the field and their variants', in U. Flick, E. von Kardorff and I. Steinke (eds), *A Companion to Qualitative Research*. London. Sage, pp. 195–202.

4
Qualitative research designs

Chapter objectives

After reading this chapter, you should

- see the role of research designs in qualitative research;
- know about what influences the construction of designs and what the components are;
- know the basic designs that can be used; and
- understand, from examples, what characterizes a good or bad design in qualitative research.

Research designs in qualitative research

The term 'research design' is less common in qualitative research than in the quantitative area, where it is the major instrument for planning research and securing the quality of its results. According to such an understanding, Ragin defines the term 'research design':

> Research design is a plan for collecting and analysing evidence that will make it possible for the investigator to answer whatever questions he or she has posed. The design of an investigation touches almost all aspects

of the research, from the minute details of data collection to the selection of the techniques of data analysis. (1994, p. 191)

That in qualitative research little importance is attached to this aspect has led Miles and Huberman (1994, p. 16) to point out that: 'Contrary to what you might have heard, qualitative research designs do exist.' However, a brief look in the literature reveals that there are several ways of understanding research design in qualitative studies. Becker et al. (1961) show in some sense a quite typical understanding of the term 'research design' in qualitative research. Although their book about their study has a chapter on 'research design', they begin it with the statement:

In one sense, our study had no design. That is, we had no well-worked-out set of hypotheses to be tested, no data-gathering instruments, purposely designed to secure information relevant to these hypotheses, no set of analytic procedures specified in advance. Insofar as the term 'design' implies these features of elaborate prior planning, our study had none. If we take the idea of design in a larger and looser sense, using it to identify those elements of order, system, and consistency our procedures did exhibit, our study had a design. We can say what this was by describing our original view of our problem, our theoretical and methodological commitments, and the way these affected our research and were affected by it as we proceeded. (p. 17)

In a similar way, Hammersley and Atkinson (1995, p. 24) argue that 'research design should be a reflexive process which operates throughout every stage of a project'.

Thus we may state at this point that there seems to be (at least in comparison to quantitative research) a more or less vague concept of research design in qualitative research, also. In some cases (e.g. Creswell, 1998), design is used in two very specific ways. On the one hand, design has to do much with choosing an approach or a tradition of qualitative research (out of five traditions the author identifies). On the other hand, in his argumentations about research (Creswell, 2003) he continuously moves between designing the study (in the above sense) and designing writings about it (proposals at the beginning or reports at the end). In other cases, research design is described as including several components. Maxwell (2005, p. 5) sees purposes, conceptual context, methods and validity as such components grouped around the central one (the research question). In his 'interactive model of research design', the term 'design' itself is not visible (see Fig. 4.1).

What seems necessary in this context is to develop a concept of research design for qualitative research that takes the different approaches mentioned above into account and gives an orientation for planning and realizing qualitative research without sticking too closely to the understanding of the term familiar from quantitative research (see also Flick, 2004a).

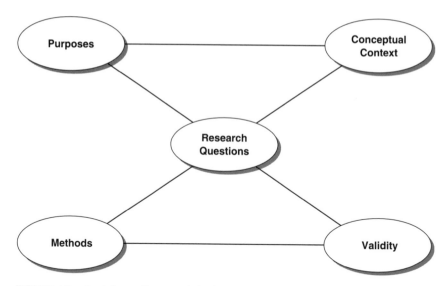

FIGURE 4.1   An interactive model of research design (Maxwell, 2005, p. 5)

Influences and components

In Chapter 2 we focused on preparatory work and planning issues preliminary to a qualitative study. We mentioned several forms of theoretical knowledge that become relevant for conceptualizing empirical, and also qualitative, research. We also addressed the fact that researchers normally adopt a specific research perspective when they approach an issue and that they should develop a research question before starting their empirical work. We spoke only briefly about the selection of methods and the fact that methods have a major influence on what is studied and the way in which it can be accessed. We will return to this point later (Chapters 8–10 below). The same is the case for available and necessary resources for doing research (see Chapter 5). All these aspects can be seen as having a major influence on how the research is planned and done in the end. They can be seen as influences on the research design developed for a study to give such planning and doing a concrete form. What is termed as 'research design' represents the sum of such influences but has direct impacts on the concrete steps of the research project that is planned and run. The influences mentioned here set up the implicit design of a qualitative study. The impacts of this implicit design and the way they are put into concrete terms make the implicit design an explicit one consisting of several components. These components are visualized as consequences in Fig. 4.2 and will be unfolded in more detail in the remainder of this chapter and this book.

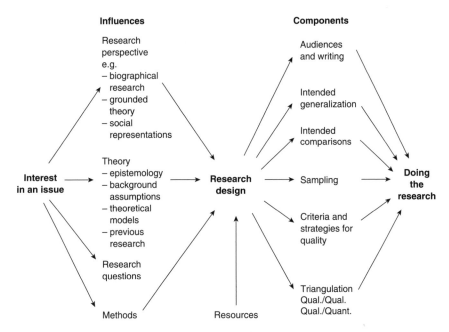

FIGURE 4.2   Constructing a research design

Components of research designs

Constructing a research design includes several components that are in some ways the result of the influences mentioned above. These components should be the result of making the research question and the research plan derived from it work.

Sampling

A central feature of every research design is sampling. In this step, researchers decide not only which material, which cases, persons or groups will be involved in a study. It also determines which comparative potential a study involves (see Chapter 3 and Merkens, 2004, for more detail).

Intended comparison

A major component of any research design is the intended comparison: which are the dimensions and levels on which you intend to draw comparisons? Is the research interested in comparing specific groups of persons (or situations) with each other? In such a study, it is not only necessary to include exemplars of each group, but also enough examples in each group so that the researcher can decide if differences (or similarities) are group- or case-specific. Furthermore, it should be considered how to include the variety in a group in such a group-comparing design.

Comparisons can be related to cases as a whole or to certain dimensions in the case – for example, to do a comparison of different cultures. In such a study, it seems necessary to include cases in the sample that are more or less comparable in many dimensions, so that differences can be linked to the different cultures. In a study on women's health concepts in Germany and Portugal, we started with the interest to see if there are indicators for cultural differences in health concepts. Therefore, we selected interview partners from both cultures and we looked for pairs of cases (in a more or less strict way). In order to be able to trace cultural differences in the interviewees' health concepts, we tried to keep as many of the other conditions in the cases as constant as possible. Therefore, the women included in the study should live under at least very similar conditions in as many respects as possible (living in a big city, having comparable professions, income and level of education), in order to be able to relate differences to the comparative dimension of 'culture' (cf. Flick, 2000a). The study was an exploratory study with a limited number of cases in each subgroup. The study had a comparative design – two groups of women were compared for a specific feature, their health and illness concepts.

In this example, comparisons were possible and could be planned on different levels if the design were adequately organized (see Fig. 4.3):

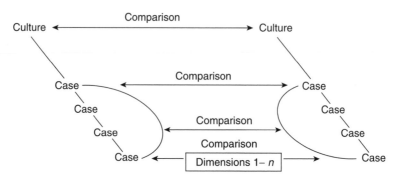

FIGURE 4.3   Levels of comparison

- Starting from the lowest level in Fig. 4.3, we could compare cases on one (or more) dimension (1–n). This comparison could be planned between cases coming from each of the (cultural) groups. For example, we could compare the definition of health given by each interviewee. Cases in this example would then be persons. We could apply such a dimensional comparison also to cases in one group.

- On a second level, we could compare the cases as cases (not reduced to a dimension), again in the group or across the groups.
- On a third level, we could make comparisons in a group among the cases and then do the same with both groups and do the final comparison between the results of this group for internal comparison.
- On a fourth level, we could make a comparison on the level of the context, in this example the cultures, looking for differences among the cases or answers coming from one or the other cultural background.

It does not make sense to plan all these forms of comparison for one study at the same time. Rather you should reflect about which level of comparison you want to address and then plan the study's design accordingly. This has implications for the step of sampling but also for the way of planning the data collection (which questions to ask to be able to draw conclusions on the level of a specific dimension, which cases to select to have 'typical' cases for a cultural comparison, etc.). Comparison often is based on contrasting cases (or events) with each other. Here, the suggestion of applying minimal and maximal contrast seems a fruitful way to give the comparisons a structure. In these strategies, you make assumptions about which cases are expected to be most similar or most different. Minimal contrasts would then look for similarities in the most similar cases, so that you can find out the core of the variation in the field. Maximal contrasts are rather interested in analyzing the differences in the most different cases, so that you can find out about the variance in the field. Of course you would look for both – differences and similarities – in both strategies, but the main focus is different in each strategy. The purpose of this sort of comparison is less to answer questions of generalization, but first of all to develop a more systematic understanding of the material you analyze and of the structures in it. Which form of comparison you should prefer is an outcome of the research design that followed from your research question and epistemological and theoretical background as well as the methods you use.

Intended generalization

Another issue that plays a major part in the construction of research is the intended level of generalization. Qualitative research often is not very strongly linked to generalization issues. Lincoln and Guba (1985, p. 110) even hold that 'the only generalization is: there is no generalization'. However, any form of research starts with a claim for generalization. Even in a case study, we assume that we can make a statement, draw a conclusion, or end up with some findings that are relevant beyond the immediate situation of data collection, if they only apply to the life of the case beyond the research situation. On the other hand, statistical generalization is neither what qualitative research provides nor what is linked as a claim to it. Therefore, it seems helpful to distinguish different forms of generalization. Maxwell, for example, distinguishes 'internal' and 'external' generalization: 'Internal generalizability refers to the generalizability of a conclusion within the setting or group studied, while external generalizability refers to its generalizability beyond that setting or group' (2005, p. 115).

The first one is also a claim for any qualitative research, whereas the second one is spelled out differently and is an issue for constructing a design. Here, we can again distinguish different goals of generalization (see Flick, 2006, chap. 12). Normally, qualitative research is aiming less at a numeric generalization than at theoretical generalization. In the case of developing a grounded theory, the claim is to have a substantive theory (applying to specific field) or a formative theory (applying to a variety of different fields) as in the case of Glaser and Strauss's (1965) theory of awareness contexts. This theory was first developed to explain a specific phenomenon (communication about the near death of a patient in a hospital) and then extended to other types of similar phenomena (e.g. communication in buying and selling used cars). These two types of theories (substantive and formative) are two forms of possible generalizations on a theoretical level. In planning the design of our research, we should think about which claim of generalization we intend to make, and how this should affect our research planning. On the other hand, we should carefully reflect which form of generality we want to reach in our research and then try to limit the range of possible dimension to be represented in the sample of our study. Do we really need a comparison according to gender, age, contexts of living such as town, countryside, city and the like? Or can we limit the relevant dimensions due to a well-defined claim of generalization?

Quality issues

In quantitative research, research design is strongly linked to assuring the quality of research mainly through standardization of the research situation. The strategy here is to control as many influences on the research situation and on the presentation of the issue under study as possible. These are ways of guaranteeing or increasing validity, reliability and objectivity (see also Flick, 2007). In qualitative research, neither these criteria nor standardization are issues treated with consensus or even as standards in research planning. Nevertheless, issues of control and a limited standardization can become important, also. In the context of comparison, we have already addressed the need to keep some features in the different cases in similar conditions in order to be able to link the observed differences to a specific feature – cultural backgrounds in the above example. In many projects, several methodological features of the research are kept constant. For example, in using semi-structured interviews the idea is included to develop an interview guide, which is then applied more or less consistently in each interview. Although often the necessary degree of freedom is more strongly focused, such a constant use of a method is expected to help to analyze the data from a comparative point of view. A constant use of a method will increase the similarity of the research situations in which the data were produced, so that differences in the data can more likely be drawn back to differences in the interviewees (their attitudes towards something, for example) rather than to the differences in the situation of data collection. In such a case, the design includes a relatively high degree of control and standardization. Miles and Huberman (1994) would see this as a tighter design in qualitative research, in which the research question is narrower and the sampling is more determined as well as the conditions of data collection. They oppose this to loose designs, in which these three features (research questions, sampling and data collection) are used more openly and flexibly. If quality issues are linked to such tightness in the design of a study, they become relevant in constructing the design and planning of the study (see also Chapter 6 and Flick, 2007, for more details).

Audiences and writing

In constructing the research design, you should reflect whom you intend to address as audiences with this research and its results. If it is an academic audience, for example a doctoral committee at a university which is to approve the results of the research as an academic qualification, for example a PhD, then the planning of the research, the running of the project and the results should be presented in a way that meets their criteria of good scientific practice. This may influence the planning of the study on a practical level (e.g. how many participants in a study are expected) but also the ways of writing about the research, which should meet standards and expectations of scientific rigour.

A different case is research addressing an audience of practitioners, who might be more interested in the practical implications of the results and less in the details of the scientific rigour that led to them. If research is intended to facilitate, support or generally influence political and administrative decisions, clarity and reduction of scientific complexity are very important for reaching this audience. Then, sometimes, methodological shortcut strategies nevertheless leading to credible results are more important than (over-) elaborate methodological finesse in the planning of the research.

These are examples of how audiences and writing can influence the planning of research in a considerable way and thus become a component of constructing a research design.

Triangulation

For many issues we may find that one methodological approach is not enough and therefore extend the design to using more than one method. In general, we can discuss this as triangulation with a focus on promoting the quality of qualitative research (see Flick, 2007). But we can also use this approach for extending

43

the knowledge we want to obtain in our study. In constructing a research design, this may have different implications on the practical level. We may be confronted with different logics of sampling in a study using triangulation – for example, sampling people for interviews and situations for observation. Triangulation can also offer new ways of comparison in a study and bring in new needs for planning such a comparison (see Flick, 2007, chap. 8 for more details). And, perhaps most importantly, triangulation will have implications for the resources necessary for the study (see Chapter 5 for more about this topic). All these issues may become practically relevant in constructing a qualitative research design, which includes several qualitative methods.

Finally, recent trends tend more to mixing qualitative and quantitative methods in one design (see Tashakkori and Teddlie, 2003a, and Flick, 2007, for more details). This becomes relevant for constructing a research design in different ways. The question of how to integrate both approaches in one design is not yet fully answered in general. In particular, when qualitative approaches are taken seriously in such a design and not just subordinated and marginalized, this has consequences for the other components in the research design: how to organize sampling so that we do not end up with a random sample of a limited number of cases for the qualitative research, but use an appropriate way of sampling for this part too. How to make sure that the quality of the research is not simply assessed according to the 'quantitative logic'. Should we simply and pragmatically mix methods or do we need a more refined and reflected combination of perspectives on the theoretical, methodological and conceptual level as in an approach of triangulation? These are questions that transform the more general approaches and problems of combining qualitative and quantitative research on the level of designing (qualitative) research.

Limiting the focus

A main feature of any good research design (not only in qualitative research) is its potential of limiting the focus of the planned study. A good research design is a precondition for breaking down a complex issue of research and a broad interest in this issue to something that can be managed in an (always) limited time with (always) limited resources and can lead to a relevant approach and results. Constructing a research design successfully means to define who or what shall be studied (and who or what shall not), what the relevant dimensions of comparison are like, and so on.

Using a basic design in qualitative research

In qualitative research, design issues are often linked to choosing a basic design for one's own study (see Creswell, 1998, or Flick, 2006, chap. 12). In discussions of research designs in general (e.g. in Bryman, 2004) we find two basic distinctions: one is between cross-sectional studies and longitudinal studies, the other between comparative and case studies. Combinations of elements of both distinctions are possible and usual. The distinction between cross-sectional and longitudinal study is based on the number of empirical contacts with the field. In a cross-sectional study, comparisons of a number of cases are mostly made on one occasion, whereas the longitudinal study returns to the field twice or more often to do the same data collection again in order to cover development and change in the field and in the issue under study. This can be transferred to qualitative research without problems, but we will find that real longitudinal studies in qualitative research are rather exceptional. 'Real' longitudinal means to start research when a process under study begins and to come back to the process repeatedly for collecting data – for example, with repeated interviews with the same people over a longer period. There are some examples of such a longitudinal research with qualitative methods (see the special issue edited by Thomson et al., 2003), but in most cases qualitative research takes a longitudinal perspective in a different way. A substitute for a prospective longitudinal research is often to take a retrospective perspective looking back on a development or process, for example in narrative or biographical study. Another alternative is to plan an observational or ethnographic study with a prolonged participation in the field for covering development over time. In the definitions of cross-sectional studies given by Bryman (2004, p. 41), cross-sectional research is strongly linked to a comparative perspective. In qualitative research, we also find studies not taking a longitudinal or retrospective perspective, but an orientation on a single point of time. Therefore, I prefer the term 'snapshot' rather than cross-sectional study for distinguishing it from more time-oriented studies (see Fig. 4.4).

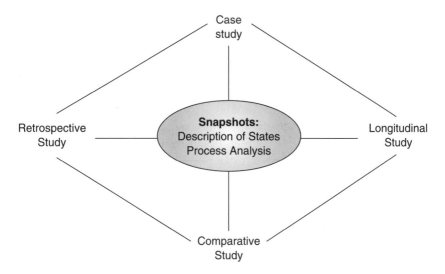

FIGURE 4.4   Basic designs in qualitative research

45

In the basic designs of qualitative research we can also distinguish case studies and comparative studies. For the former, the relevant question is how to define the case and its limits: first it will be the research question, which gives an answer to this. But then we find a very wide range of conceptualizations of what a case is (see the contributions to Ragin and Becker, 1992).

If we study cases, we can see a person, an institution (such as his or her family), an organization (where he or she works), a community (where he or she lives) or an event (that he or she has experienced) as a case, depending on the topic and the research question of our study. These examples are meant to demonstrate that 'cases' in case studies are not necessary persons. If we take a person as a case, we can think about which of the units just mentioned are relevant for understanding the case – maybe we need to integrate the whole family in studying the case of a pupil failing at school, perhaps we need to integrate the school in our study.

In a comparative study, the most relevant issues are to define the dimension of comparison and how to take the context of the cases in the study into account (see above).

The different basic designs of qualitative research discussed so far can be related along two axes (see Fig. 4.4): along the dimension of time (from retrospective to snapshot and longitudinal study) and along the dimension of case vs. comparative studies. In the research practice, we will find combinations from both dimensions, for example retrospective case studies as well as retrospectives studies with a comparative perspective.

Examples of qualitative research designs

In what follows, some examples of research designs will be outlined in order to show how they were developed and which decisions were taken in this process.

Health concepts of professionals

With this example, I want to show how a rather comprehensive and complex research interest (relevance of concepts from new public health for professional practice) and research perspective (social representations of health and illness – see Fig. 2.1 in Chapter 2) could be turned into a relatively focused research design (see Fig. 4.5). Which were the relevant decisions guiding the construction of this design?

The first decision was to do a comparative study – in this case to include two professional groups. The second decision was to take those professional groups for the study who are at the border of the health system and everyday life and

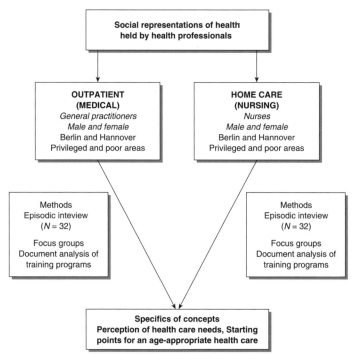

FIGURE 4.5   Research design: professionals' concepts of health

therefore have a gatekeeper position for people feeling a more or less concrete need for professional support. The third decision was to take a medical and a non-medical profession. All three decisions led to choosing general practitioners on the medical side due to their gatekeeper function and home-care nurses due to their work on the border between a private and an institutional life for older people with health problems. Finally, we decided to take two cities in Germany with a similar social structure – in our case Berlin and Hanover. In both cities, we were interested in professionals working in more privileged areas and in socially weaker areas. Furthermore, we intended to have male and female participants in both professional groups, since one (nurses) is a traditionally female profession whereas the other (doctors) is more dominated by men. These decisions led to setting up subsamples of 16 participants in each city and profession, so that we ended up with 64 interviews, 32 in each profession, 32 in each city, half men and half women. As we wanted to see developments in the professional practice of our interviewees, we were looking for participants working in their field for at least five years.

In addition to these sampling decisions, we included a combination of several methodological approaches. The main approach was to use the episodic interview (Flick, 2000b, 2007) for having a more narrative and a more conceptual approach to experiences of the participants in their practice. This was triangulated with focus groups (see Barbour, 2007) towards the end of the project, for which we recruited those of the interviewees who were ready to take part in another step of the research (see more about triangulation in Flick, 2007). The intention of this second step was to give the participants a feedback of the results of the interviews and their analysis and to stimulate a discussion about this feedback and then to take these discussions as a second source of data for the final analysis. A third methodological approach was to analyze documents about the representation of the issues studied in the interviews and focus groups. The documents included here were curricula of training programs in both professions over the period when our participants had passed their professional training.

The project was funded for two years. The funding allowed employing two full-time researchers and two student researchers.

In this example the research design was based on sampling decisions (whom to interview), selection of sites (two professional fields; two local areas with two different social settings each – high and low status areas) and definition of features for comparison (gender, professional experience) in each subgroup. Nevertheless, the claim for generalization was limited – there was no intention to see this sample as representative of general practitioners or nurses in general. In some ways, this study can be seen as a case study trying to explore how certain concepts and topics find their way into practices with selecting fields and participants purposefully (see Fig. 4.5 for the research design of the study).

Health of homeless adolescents

In a second example, we had a less comparative perspective in mind than in the first example. Here it was rather a very special group that was the focus of the study: we were interested in health concepts and experiences of homeless adolescents in a German city. Our study addresses several aspects summarized in two main research questions: Which representations of health do homeless adolescents hold? And which forms of health practices are reported or can be observed? The study is conducted in a German city and includes 24 homeless adolescents (12 female and 12 male aged 14–20 years, see Table 4.1), who regularly hang out

TABLE 4.1 Sample according to age and gender

Age (in years)	Gender		
	Male (N = 12)	Female (N = 12)	Total (N = 24)
14–17	5	9	14
18–20	7	3	10
Ø	17.5	16.0	16.75

at specific public spots. To find access to homeless adolescents in order to interview them, the researcher participated in social street work and in a low barrier drop-in centre for the target group. Adolescents met in this context were informed about the purpose of this research and contributed to making this project known among their peers so that it hardly raised any suspicion. The drop-in centre was used for making appointments with the adolescents in a room free of external disturbances. The adolescents were asked for their concepts of health and their experiences of health, health problems and how they deal with them. They were asked to recount situations referring to such experiences. The interview guide included several topics: how interviewees turned to street life; their subjective definitions of health; their current situation (housing, financial problems, nutrition) and its consequences for health; and how they handle health problems and risks (drugs, alcohol, sexuality). Participant observation in the peer groups complemented the interviews in order to understand the health practices of the interviewees and their peers. The project was funded for 18 months and this allowed employing one full-time researcher.

All in all, this again is not a study claiming representativeness of the sample or of the results. It is an example of an exploratory study with a marginalized group not addressed by research (in Germany at least) on a sensitive topic and asking for sensitive answers from the participants. The difficulties of finding access and the lack of previous research to build on are major justifications for using qualitative methods in this study. Here, the design was again the result of a series of decisions: what to understand as homeless (here having stayed for a minimum time without regular shelter, but not necessarily rough sleeping permanently); what to understand as adolescents (here age 14 to 20 years); where to localize homelessness and hanging out in public places. First we wanted to take two areas with different kinds of homeless people and to compare both areas, but when the project started, one of the areas – a train station – was rebuilt, so the scene had gone and we had to concentrate on one area. Again we were interested in gender differences, so we planned half of the sample to be female. Sampling decisions followed a decision for a specific site, including institutions offering support for our target group and supporting the research by facilitating access to the field and the participants. The methodological part of the design included again a triangulation of two methods, this time of interviewing and participant observation in an ethnographic access (see Angrosino, 2007; Kvale, 2007).

What characterizes a good qualitative research design?

If we want to draw some conclusions from this chapter and think about the features of a good research design in qualitative research, the following characteristics may be noted.

A good design has a *clear focus* and is built around *a clear research question*. Both design and questions allow the research to *reduce* the study *to the essential* issue for answering the question. A good design makes the research *manageable in resources and time* and is clear in *decisions about sampling* and *why particular methods are used*. It is also *well linked to the theoretical background* and *based on the research perspective* of the study. Finally, it reflects the aims of generalization and the audiences of the study and, more concretely, it allows doing the comparisons that are intended in the study. Seen in this way, a good research design is the result of reflection, planning and clear decisions about the steps of constructing a design, which were discussed in this chapter. However, a good design should at the same time be *sensitive, flexible and adaptive* to conditions in the field, and in this be *open to new insights* resulting from the first steps or during the progress of the research.

Key points

- Qualitative research may profit from developing or using a research design as well.
- There are several influences on the construction of qualitative research.
- Qualitative research desgins consist of many components and can be based on a basic design.
- A major function for a research design is to reduce the focus of the research.

Further reading

In the following books, the issue of designing qualitative research is unfolded in more detail:

Flick, U. (2006) *An Introduction to Qualitative Research* (3rd ed.). London: Sage.

Flick, U. (2007) *Managing Quality in Qualitative Research* (Book 8 of *The SAGE Qualitative Research Kit*). London: Sage.

Marshall, C. and Rossman, G.B. (2006) *Designing Qualitative Research* (4th ed.). Thousand Oaks, CA: Sage.

Maxwell, J.A. (2005) *Qualitative Research Design – An Interactive Approach* (2nd ed.). Thousand Oaks, CA: Sage.

Miles, M.B. and Huberman, A.M. (1994) *Qualitative Data Analysis: A Sourcebook of New Methods* (2nd ed.). Newbury Park, CA: Sage.

5
Resources and stepping-stones

Chapter objectives
After reading this chapter, you should

- know more about how to calculate a research project on the level of resources like time, money and skills; and
- see some of the stepping-stones that you may be confronted with once you enter the field and try to make your research plan work.

Introduction

In the preceding chapter, we mentioned that a good research design is characterized by a reasonable calculation and use of existing resources. In this chapter, we will focus on how to calculate and plan resources not only in a funded qualitative project in order to end up with a reasonable budget.

Resources

Something frequently undervalued in the development of a research design are the available or necessary resources (time, personnel, technical support, competences, experience and so on). Research proposals are often based on an unrealistic relationship between the planned tasks and the personnel resources that can (realistically) be asked for.

Time and technical resources

For realistic project planning, I suggest making a calculation of the activities involved. This calculation may refer to the overall time-scale of a project (see below) or to planning the single activities in the project. So you should take into account, for example, that an interview of around 90 minutes will need as much time again for locating interview partners, organizing appointments, and travel. For the calculation of time necessary for transcribing interviews, the estimates will diverge widely, depending on the precision of the system of transcription you want to use. Morse (1994, pp. 232–3) suggests that, for fast-writing transcribers, the length of the tape containing the interview recording be multiplied by a factor of 4. If checking the finished transcript against the tape is also included, the length of the tape should be multiplied by a total of 6. For the complete calculation of the project she suggests that the time allowed be doubled to allow for unforeseen difficulties and 'catastrophes'. If you take a refined transcription system (Jeffersonian transcription: Rapley, 2007, or Kvale, 2007), the necessary time will grow considerably. A more pragmatic suggestion for transcribing interviews, for example, is given in Box 5.1. If you use these suggestions for transcribing your interviews, transcripts like the one in Box 5.2 should

Box 5.1	Rules for transcription
Layout:	
Word processor	Word (97 or later)
Font	Times New Roman 12
Margin	left 2, right 5
Line numbers	5, 10, 15, etc., every page starts again
Lines	1.5
Page numbers	On top, right
Interviewer:	I: Interviewer
Interviewee:	IP: Interviewee
Transcription:	
Spelling	Conventional
Punctuation	Conventional

Breaks	Short break: * more than 1 sec: *no of seconds*
Incomprehensible parts	((incomp))
Uncertain transcription	(abc)
Loud	With commentary
Low	With commentary
Emphasis	With commentary
Break off word	Abc-
Break off sentence	Abc-
Simultaneous talk	#abc#
Paralinguistic utterance	With commentary (e.g. sighs ...)
Commentary	With commentary
Verbatim quote	Conventional
Abbreviations	Conventional
Anonymization	Names with °

Box 5.2   Example from a transcript   1

I: Yeah the first question is, what is this for you, health? ((telephone rings)) Do you want to pick it up first?

N: No.

I: No? Okay.

5 N: Health is relative, I think. Someone can be healthy, too, who is old and has a handicap and can feel healthy nevertheless. Well, in earlier times, before I came to work in the community, I always said, someone is healthy if he lives in a very well ordered household, where everything is correct and super exact, and I would like to say, absolutely clean? But I learnt better, when I started to work in the community

10 (...). I was a nurse in the Hanover Medical School before that, in intensive care and arrived here with. ...

I = Interviewer; N = Nurse

result. To keep the transcription to the minimum that is necessary for answering the research question can be an important decision in planning a project in a limited time-scale.

The time needed for data interpretation is more difficult to calculate. Sample plans of how to calculate the time parameters of empirical projects are to be found in Marshall and Rossman (2006, chap. 6).

In Box 5.3, an example for a time-scale for a qualitative study using interviews and participant observation is reproduced (it comes from our study on homeless adolescents' health concepts). Such a time-scale can have two functions: in a proposal in the application for funding, it will demonstrate how much time is needed and for what purpose in order to convince the funding agency that a budget you ask for is justified. In designing the research, the time-scale will give you an orientation in the planning of the project.

In the process of approving a project the equipment asked for is sometimes reduced and additional methodological stages, such as an additional group for comparison or phase of data collection, may be required. At this stage, if not before, it becomes essential to check the relationship between tasks and resources, and shortcut strategies in the methodological procedures should be considered if necessary.

In planning a project that will work with transcribed interviews (or other forms of recorded data), a high-quality tape recorder should always be used for the recordings, and a special instrument with a foot-operated switch is essential for transcription.

If a decision is taken to use computers and programs such as ATLAS, MAXQda and NUDIST (see Gibbs, 2007) for data interpretation, then it is essential to include in the plan sufficient time for technical preparation (installation, removal of errors, instruction of team members in the use of the program, and so on).

Money

Here we can distinguish three sorts of costs to be taken into account. First, in a funded or commissioned project, you should plan enough *salaries or payment* for the people working in the project according to the numbers of working hours you need to do the project. So you might calculate that you need one full-time researcher for two years and one part-time researcher for the period of data collection and analysis as support. For calculating how many working hours you may need for the project, see the section on time calculation above. If, for example, the transcription is to be done by the people working in the project, you should calculate enough time for doing so. How much money per working hour or per month of employment you should calculate depends on the local context in which you prepare your project.

Box 5.3 Time-scale for a project

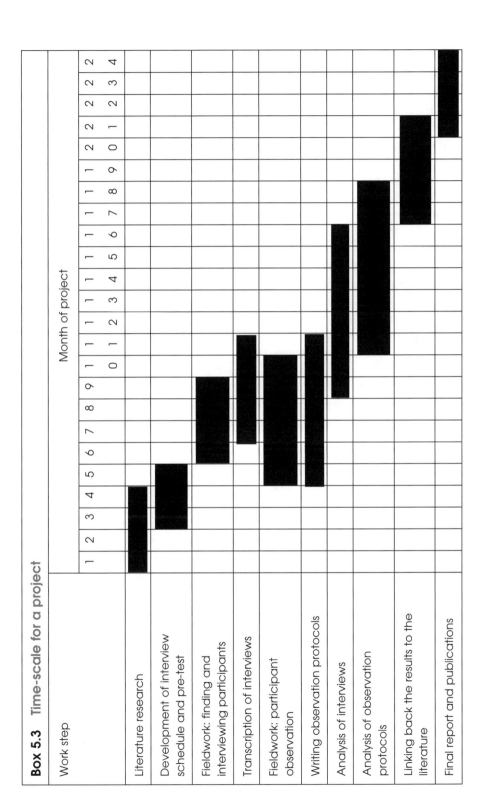

A second type of cost are *operating costs* for a qualitative study, which will arise whether or not the project is based on funded employment of the researchers or is a dissertation project without funding. Here we can mention the costs for technical equipment that is not already available: good recording equipment, computers, software (word processing and, if used, CAQDAS software like ATLAS/ti), a tape recorder supporting the transcription, tapes, paper, printer and ink, video camera, recorder and screen if video is to be used, costs for photo-copies and the like. In some cases you will have to pay for data collection – for example, if you have to buy documents for analyzing them (like a year of a news-paper). Sometimes, costs for doing interviews will arise, like paying the intervie-wees for the time spent, or refunding their travel to your office or for paying your travel to them. If you decide to give away transcription you have to calculate how much you will have to pay the transcribers per page (or hour) and how many units (pages, hours) you expect to accrue.

Third, *dissemination costs* may need to be calculated: travelling to conferences where you plan to present results will produce costs (travel, fees for the confer-ence, etc.). Printing a report or paying a publisher for printing a book with your results may consume some money, also.

Table 5.1 gives an orientation for calculating the costs of a project in a three-year plan. The figures to fill in would result from your individual project's needs and the conditions under which you will have to work (what is the regular salary for a researcher per year or per month, what kind of equipment you need, and what it will cost where your project is located, etc.).

Experience and skills

Another resource is the necessary skills for doing the project. Thus an impor-tant step in preparing your research project is to become experienced in using the methods you want to apply, especially under two conditions: first, if you decide to use a (for yourself) new methodology, which you will apply for the first time; second, if you use a method you have applied before, but with new members in the team who have not yet done qualitative research or research with this method. In these cases, you should prepare the application of the methods in your project. For example, in interview training, all the members of the research team practice the use of the interview guide in role-plays. The other members watch them, do a video recording of the role-play and analyze it for giving feedback to the person who played the role of the interviewer. In turn everybody will take the role of the interviewer, so that differences in asking questions, in probing, in non-verbal behaviour towards the interviewee, etc., can be reflected. This gives experiences with the interview situation and allows some kind of comparability of the situations and research behaviours in the team at the same time. Such a preparation was

TABLE 5.1   Model of a form for calculating the costs of a qualitative project

Budget item	Year 1	Year 2	Year 3
Salaries etc.			
Salaries for researcher(s)			
Transcription costs			
Payment for interviewees			
Operating costs			
Equipment (technical, computers, recording devices, software)			
Rents, furniture			
Materials			
Printing			
Travel costs			
For data collection			
Conferences			
Meetings			
Other costs			
......			
......			

helpful in preparing the interviews with the doctors and nurses in our project mentioned above.

Some of the costs will not arise in every project, some of the equipment is already available in your institution and can be used, sometimes you will not apply for funding or have researchers paid as extra costs, but do the research by your own in the framework of a dissertation, for example. But for a full financing and planning, the costs mentioned above should be taken into account in order to avoid unpleasant surprises with running out of time and resources.

Stepping-stones

Planning and designing qualitative research is one thing, doing it in the field and with real people is another. In the next step, I want to address some of the stepping-stones that may complicate making a research design work in the field.

Special problems and stepping-stones linked to using specific methods will be taken up in Chapters 8–10 of this book.

Finding no access

Of course it is not possible in this context to foresee all the problems that might arise (but see Wolff, 2004, for some of them). But we can distinguish two sorts of problems here: for research in institutions, you have often to contact several levels of administrative decision-makers before you can get in touch with your research participants. Each of these levels can have reservations against research in the institution in general or your research (topic, purpose, effects, etc.) in particular. On each of the levels, you have to negotiate your entry to the field. Wolff (2004, p. 199) describes a repertoire of strategies in institutions to avoid decisions for and against a research inquiry. Here we find strategies of 'wait and see', passing the inquiry and the decision to the next (higher) level in the hierarchy, and the like. In each case, you will have to negotiate and respond to the suggestions or demands formulated by your counterparts. Once your research has been formally approved by the institution, you will have to find access to the 'right' – i.e. relevant, experienced, informative, etc. – persons to convince them to take part in your research (e.g. by giving you an interview). Sometimes you will meet specific reservations against one method or the other in some people (who do not like to be interviewed), while others will have no problems with the same request. Here, you have to keep in mind what it means for your sampling if you just include those people in your study who have the fewest reservations (Patton, 2002, speaks of convenience sampling in this context and discusses the problems of this strategy).

If you plan your research in an open field, access may be complicated for different reasons. In particular, if you want to work with people difficult to find or access (hidden populations, vulnerable people), you often have to approach institutions working with these people in order to find them. Here, you are often confronted with gatekeepers who for one reason or another are concerned about the effects of your research on the participants and want to protect them by not letting you get in touch with them. Such protective engagements may sometimes be necessary and justified, but it can make your research more difficult even if it was good for possible participants to be involved. In such a case, you should be ready to have arguments for such gatekeepers why your research is not only important for you but also for your participants. However, you should be careful not to make promises you may have trouble in keeping later. In the example of our homeless adolescents and health project, we may produce results that can be used for improving support for this group by the health institutions. But before such an improvement can be effective, the single participants of our study may no longer profit from it – for example, because they are no longer adolescents. Having found access to the people you want to interview does not necessarily mean they are open to your question and to you as a person. Access and entry have a lot to do with positioning yourself as a person to be trusted as a partner in dialogues, as being confidential and trustworthy and as someone competent in what you are doing or planning to do.

Matching methods and fields

In this context it is also important to reflect what you can expect from your field and your participants. Perhaps if you have developed an elaborate design, including different methods to be applied repeatedly, you will find out that this over-challenges your participants. If your potential interview partners face a tight time schedule (in their work, for example), you should reflect whether your interview planning will fit into such a schedule or should be planned to be shorter, for example. Sometimes it is difficult to find a room in which you can do an interview without interruptions by others, if you do your research in an open field, and it may be unlikely that your potential interviewees can travel to your institution for an interview. In such cases, you will have to adapt your design and methods to what is possible in the field or you will have trouble ending up with a sufficient number of interviews (with relevant people) when your project time becomes short.

Neglecting the participants' perspective

It is also important to reflect what your participants expect from being part in your research. Sometimes it is a specific form of attention they look for. Sometimes they may think they have something important to say beyond your topic. In such a case, you should try to be open about what information they have to offer beyond answering your questions and you should try to be flexible in the contact so that you can register this offer. Without losing the focus on your research interest, you should try to take your participants and their perspective seriously in your contact with them.

Associations instead of analysis

In an interview study, you will receive a lot of interesting statements. In participant observation, you will see a lot of interesting things you did not expect and so on. In analyzing these data, it is important to keep a theoretical and critical perspective on what you obtained and to scrutinize what was presented to you. You should try to be systematic in what you do with the data and not just associate to what was said, but develop structures in and from the data – for example, typologies – or identify patterns in them. This will make it more likely that you find out something about the field you study, which was not yet known – to its members, to other scientists, and maybe to yourself beforehand.

Conclusion

The lists of necessary resources and even more of possible stepping-stones presented in this chapter are not exhaustive. But both can give you a first orientation of what to keep in mind while designing your research. They will be complemented in more detail in the chapters addressing methods (8–10) and in the other books of *The SAGE Qualitative Research Kit*.

≡ Key points

- Doing qualitative research is based on having different kinds of resources available.
- It is important to do a sound calculation of these resources in qualitative research when applying for funding or when you estimate the needs for your project.
- Major stepping-stones in qualitative research are linked to finding access and to making the methods fit to conditions in the field.

Further reading

In the following works, the resources and stepping-stones in qualitative research are discussed in more detail:

Flick, U. (2006) *An Introduction to Qualitative Research* (3rd ed.). London: Sage.
Marshall, C. and Rossman, G.B. (2006) *Designing Qualitative Research* (4th ed.). Thousand Oaks, CA: Sage
Maxwell, J.A. (2005) *Qualitative Research Design – An Interactive Approach* (2nd ed.). Thousand Oaks, CA: Sage.
Wolff, S. (2004) 'Ways into the field and their variants', in U. Flick, E. von Kardorff and I. Steinke (eds), *A Companion to Qualitative Research*. London: Sage, pp. 195–202.

6
Quality in qualitative research

Chapter objectives
After reading this chapter, you should

- see how quality issues in qualitative research are relevant in planning the research, and in doing and reporting it;
- know about the different levels on which quality will be defined and influenced on each of the three steps; and
- have an orientation for the later chapters, where quality issues are focused on methods.

Introduction

In standardized research, quality is one of the major issues in constructing a research design, perhaps the major issue. Quality in that context is closely linked to standardization and control of the research situation and over influences on it. The basic idea then is that if we manage to control and exclude disturbing influences – coming from the outside or from researchers' bias – we can find access to the issue under study in an unbiased way and represent it in the results in a valid, reliable and objective way. Standardization of the research situation and making it independent from the single researcher, who applies the questionnaire or does the experiment, is then the *via regia* to research quality.

In qualitative research, discussions about quality in research are not so much based on the idea of standardization and control, as this seems incompatible with many of the methods used here. Quality is rather seen as an issue of how to manage it (see Flick, 2007). Sometimes it is linked to rigour in applying a certain method, but more often to soundness of the research as a whole. This makes the research process the point of reference for quality issues and at the same time makes quality an issue for designing qualitative research again in three respects: in designing qualitative research on the level of planning research; in doing qualitative research on the levels of field contacts and analyzing qualitative data; and in disseminating qualitative research to audiences and participants. As the latter two activities are strongly based on the first and have an impact on designing and planning qualitative research, they will be discussed here as well.

Designing qualitative research with quality

In the planning of qualitative research, there are several starting points for developing, improving and assuring, or (briefly summarized) promoting quality in the research.

Indication

First of all, quality in qualitative research (planning) is based on a clear, explicit and reflected decision for a specific method (see Chapters 8–10) or design (see Chapter 4). This can be summarized in the question of indication of my research procedures (see Flick, 2007, chap. 10). It should be obvious in the planning of the project that the decision for qualitative research in general, for a specific approach within it and for a concrete method was not based on a general sympathy or attitude towards these. Indication of methods, approaches, designs and research types should be based on reflection of the issue under study, the research question linked to it, the existing knowledge of the issue and the population (see Flick, 2007, Table 10.1). If all these components justify the use of a specific method, design or approach, we can speak of indication in this context. That a method, design or approach is indicated can be an important condition for the quality of its use and the project as a whole.

In the example of our project on professionals' health concepts, the indication for the episodic interview was based first on the lack of similar research, which became clear from studying the literature. It was also based on our assumptions about the knowledge we were interested to study: it could be expected that the professionals' knowledge about the relevance of health and prevention in their day-to-day practices would consist of concepts (what is health, what is prevention?) and memories from situations in which they used it (or not). The research question (see Chapter 2) demanded a method addressing conceptual knowledge and representations of changes and developments. This population would be prepared to answer questions and recount situations as expected in using the episodic interview. A combination with focus groups for feeding back the results to practical contexts seemed to promise additional insights on a different level – evaluations of results and implications coming from a group.

Adequacy

Whereas indication refers to the decision for specific methods, adequacy means that you check and recheck whether a specific method or design fits your research issue and field. If necessary, this would mean redesigning your study in order to make your choices adequate to what you want to study and where. More concretely, adequacy as an approach to quality means that you prepare the application of your methods as well as possible. You and your research team should become familiar with the methods you intend to apply. You also should do an interview or observation training before you approach your 'real' cases. In this training, you should not only have the method as such in focus, but also the issue and the people you want to study with it. A point to assess in evaluating such training could be, is the individual interviewer ready to use the method according to the rules and criteria developed for its use? A second point could be, what does that mean for the participant? Let us take as an example that you intend to study illness experiences by collecting life histories of patients in narrative interviews (see for this also Flick, 2006, chap. 14). Then you could analyze a preliminary interview for how the interviewer manages to listen to such a life story and to support the interviewee in continuing to tell it. But you should also analyze it for what it means for an interviewee to present such a life history in a narrative, and whether both are adequate for what you intend with your study.

Openness for diversity

In planning your study, you will be busy reducing the multiplicity in your research issue to a manageable research question and design. But at the same time, an indicator for the quality of a qualitative study is often how the researchers manage diversity in their design (see Flick, 2007, chap. 3) How is the search for the variety of possible experiences implemented in the research design? How do the researchers foresee handling deviant cases? How will they look for critical comments by members and other researchers? These approaches to increasing and taking into account the diversity in the field can become relevant not only in running the study, but also in planning and preparing it.

These are three approaches to addressing the quality of qualitative research already in the process of designing the research plan of the study. How far that leads to a study that can be characterized by (high) quality in the end, depends on how this planning is put into practice in the next step.

Doing qualitative research with quality

Quality of qualitative research is not (only) produced in planning and designing the study. Quality is rather produced in the making of the research. Here we can find different approaches for assessing quality. As we will see in what follows, it well be less the strict criteria than the dealing with certain tensional fields in doing qualitative research that is decisive in the end.

Rigour and creativity

In attempts to define the quality of qualitative research, for example in criteria catalogues and checklists (see Flick, 2007, for details), we regularly come across rigour in using methods, applying approaches and designs as an essential for such a definition. Rigour means that you are strict and consequent in applying a method, that you will keep to your sampling scheme and that you analyze your data without being awkward at different points. The quality of a qualitative study may build on such a methodological strictness and consequence. But it will need more to be a really good study. Here, we should mention the creativity in using the methods, in exploring the fields in taking up new insights and perspectives and in adapting the methods and plans to what fits the field. A good qualitative study will not be limited to finding and confirming what was expected to be the result, but will produce new insights and ways of seeing the things and persons that have been studied. This means that quality in qualitative research is developed and produced in the tensional field of (theoretical, conceptual, practical and methodological) creativity and (methodological) rigour in studying the phenomena, processes and people.

Consistency and flexibility

If you want to study several cases, it can be helpful and necessary for comparison to maintain a minimum of consistency. For example, in an interview study we should try to ask the same questions to all of our participants, to ask questions in a similar way to all of them and not to leave out a relevant topic or question in some of the cases. To facilitate this is the aim of developing and using an interview guide. Consistency of the researcher in this way can be discussed for other methods as well.

However, this again is only one side of the coin. Interviews may be easier to compare if they are done in a consistent way, but very good interviews always profit from the flexibility of the researchers to adapt their questions to the individual participant and to the course of the concrete interview. In ethnography, the flexible use of methods is even a criterion in itself (Lüders, 2004b, or Hammersley and Atkinson, 1995). The same can be said for developing categories and for building links between data, pieces and cases. Thus, again, quality is located in a tensional field – between being consistent and being flexible – and cannot be reduced to a sort of 'right' application of a method. How far the researchers can get along with this tension in a sovereign way depends very much on how far it was taken into account in designing and planning the study.

Criteria and strategies

Coming back to what is the major issue of research design in standardized research, we find a third tensional field in qualitative research quality. There have been numerous suggestions for defining criteria for distinguishing good from bad qualitative research. These were based on using the traditional social science criteria (reliability, validity, objectivity) here, also. We can also note suggestions for how to reformulate them (e.g. to validate is to question: Kvale, 2007) or suggestions for new criteria (e.g. credibility: Lincoln and Guba, 1985). These suggestions have so far not led to any sort of consensus as to which criteria might be the adequate ones for qualitative research or for specific areas in qualitative research. A more general problem is that these criteria do not come with benchmarks defining, for example, how much credibility should be given as a minimum for seeing a project as good qualitative research (as would be the case in assessing the intercoder reliability in quantitative research, which has to be beyond a certain percentage of corresponding coding to be acceptable).

At the same time, we can find a number of strategies for promoting the quality of qualitative research. The range here includes triangulation, analytic induction or more generally taking into account the negative case, quality management in the research process and the like (see Flick, 2007, for an overview of both discussions). Using these strategies can make a considerable contribution to improving the quality of qualitative research and this will affect the design of a concrete study. But they will not lead to clear-cut borders between good and bad research.

As these brief remarks should make clear, we should not expect a clear and universal solution to the quality question on the level of criteria in qualitative research. Rather we will continue to move in a third tensional field here – between applying criteria if possible and reasonable and using strategies for promoting quality in the research process. This tensional field will again have an impact on the design of a qualitative study and will be prepared by the concrete design decisions.

Disseminating qualitative research

In qualitative research, the quality of a piece of research only becomes assessable on the basis of the report about it:

> The research report with its presentation of and reflection on the methodological proceedings, with all its narratives about access to and the activities in the field, with its documentation of various materials, with

its transcribed observations and conversations, interpretations and theoretical inferences is the only basis for answering the question of the quality of the investigation. (Lüders, 1995, p. 325)

If we take this seriously, the question of dissemination of research and its find-ings will become relevant for judging the quality of qualitative research in three respects, which again will influence the design of a study or a project.

Transparency

In writing about our research, we should make transparent how we proceeded and how we arrived at our findings and conclusions. This is a suggestion repeatedly made for increasing the quality of qualitative research. To take it seriously means to present the project and the results in a way that allows the reader to understand how decisions (about methods, about types in typology, etc.) have been taken, how the researchers worked with deviant cases, how the analysis led to more gen-eral patterns and the like. A transparent presentation of a piece of qualitative research will not be limited to the results, but will allow the reader to develop a feeling for how the process advanced, how ideas were developed, which ideas were pursued and which were left aside. Readers should be given enough infor-mation to decide whether they would have done the same and arrived at the same conclusions as the researchers or not.

Feedback and member checks

A second feature of good practice in this context is whether the researcher has sought feedback from the field in two respects. One is the field under study. Here, steps like communicative validation, feedback loops or member checks can give important information for checking the accuracy and adequacy of the research. The second is the field of science. Did the researchers look for feedback from their colleagues? Have preliminary results been made public in conferences or journal papers? How were the reactions to them taken into account in the further research? This can also be understood as a way to manage diversity in the quali-tative research project, in this case by taking outside perspectives into account (see Flick, 2007, chap. 3).

Audiencing the presentations

This is a relevant issue already for planning the research. Who are the audiences to be addressed by the results and by the research in general? How should a report or an article be written so that it will reach its audience and be accessible for its readers? If we write for academic audiences, our style will be different from when we write for readers in a practice context, who want to draw conclusions on a practical level from our results. Finally, if our research aims at having an impact on political decision processes, we need a different style of writing again. In the latter case, we need to write in a brief style with clear indications of the most important findings and their meaning, without confusing our readers with too many details. In the first case, it is more the details that are important for classifying the results and for assessing their relevance.

On the level of disseminating the results beyond the research project and context, three issues are relevant: that you make your research transparent; that you carefully reflect if and how you transport your results back to the field and then what you do with the response from the field; and finally, that you reflect how to write for specific audiences and in general so that you reach the audience you want to address with your results and reports.

Conclusion

Quality issues become relevant for designing qualitative research on three levels, which are interlinked. If you understand qualitative research design as a reflexive planning of what you want to do in the field, what you expect to find there and how to analyze it, these three levels will influence your decisions in the planning phase.

▰▰▰ Key points

- Quality in qualitative research is the result of efforts in planning, conducting and reporting qualitative research.
- All three steps become relevant for designing qualitative research.
- In designing qualitative research, you should know why and how you would do what you plan.
- In conducting the research, quality will be developed in the context of three tensional fields.
- Dissemination of research is important as the step that connects your results back to the field, to audiences and readers in general.

Further reading

These three books will give you some more information about how to address issues of quality in qualitative research:

Flick, U. (2007) *Managing Quality in Qualitative Research* (Book 8 of *The SAGE Qualitative Research Kit*). London: Sage.

Patton, M.Q. (2002) *Qualitative Evaluation and Research Methods* (3rd ed.). London: Sage.

Seale, C. (1999) *The Quality of Qualitative Research*. London: Sage.

7
Ethics in qualitative research

Chapter objectives

After reading this chapter, you should

*   see the ethical issues that become relevant for designing qualitative research;
*   know for each step of the research process what is relevant from the angle of qualitative research ethics; and
*   be ready to break down the more general principles of qualitative research ethics to the concrete step-by-step decisions in designing qualitative research.

Introduction

The awareness of ethical issues and concerns has grown considerably in the last decades in qualitative research also (see Punch, 1994; Hopf, 2004; Christian, 2005). The discussion about ethics in research in general has been pushed forward from different angles. A number of examples have raised the awareness of research done with people not knowing about being researched and sometimes suffering from the research (medical experiments in the concentration camps during the Nazi regime in Germany but also the Tuskegee Syphilis Study, for example); the Milgram experiment, in which people were made to give other people electric shocks not knowing that they were part of a different experiment and that they were exposed to influences; cases of manipulated data and results coming up repeatedly; covert research in subgroups like the study of Humphreys (1975); and publications of ethnographic research that allowed the identification of people or communities despite attempts at anonymization. Finally, in natural sciences in particular, we have had several cases of manipulating or faking data and results in recent years.

Such cases of misuse of research and the public attention they attracted have led to establishing precautions against such violations of good practice in research. One is that most academic societies have formulated their codes of ethics (e.g. the American Sociological Association Code of Ethics, www.asanet.org, or the Statement of Ethical Practices of the British Sociological Association, www.britsoc.co.uk). The other is that most institutions doing research, such as universities, now have institutional review boards or ethics committees that have to approve a project if it involves human subjects as research partners. In principle, such institutionalized precautions are an important step towards avoiding unethical research, but as many authors show for the qualitative or field research, such institutions do not always address the 'real' problems of research and in some cases make research impossible rather than better. Also, the ethical problems in qualitative research run throughout the whole process of designing and then doing it.

There are several basic principles of ethically sound research (see also Christian, 2005, pp. 144–6):

- Informed consent means that no one should be involved in research as a participant without knowing about this and without having the chance of refusing to take part.
- Deception of research participants (by covert observation or by giving them false information about the purpose of research) should be avoided.
- Participants' privacy should be respected and confidentiality should be guaranteed and maintained.
- Accuracy of the data and their interpretation should be the leading principle, which means that no omission or fraud with the collection or analysis of data should occur in the research practice.
- In relation to the participants, respect for the person is seen as essential.
- Beneficence, which means considering the well-being of the participants.
- Justice, which addresses the relation of benefits and burdens for the research participants.

For all these principles, we can state that they are correct and important as an orientation for planning research with responsibility and care. However, they do not protect the researcher in the field from the ethical dilemmas linked to working with people in natural settings.

In this chapter, we will address ethical issues that become relevant in planning and designing a qualitative study. The aim is less to give a comprehensive overview of qualitative research ethics (see for more details Flick, 2006, chap. 4; 2007, chap. 9). Rather this chapter is intended to focus on the ethical issues that arise in the steps of the research process, planning and design.

Preparation

Reflection of ethics is not only relevant while you are in the field and it is not only something to work on while you prepare a proposal – for the ethics committee or the institutional review board of your institution. Ethics should play a role in your considerations of how to plan a study, of who you want to work with, and how you (or your fieldworkers) should act in the field.

Relevance

In preparing your project, you should reflect several issues for their ethical dimensions. The first is relevance in various respects. Is your topic already 'over-researched'? Is there enough research already done and will your research contribute something new to the existing stock of knowledge?

Participants

When you think about your possible participants, is it justifiable to expose them to your research, especially if you intend to work with vulnerable people like children, patients, very old people or those living under difficult circumstances? This does not mean that you should do no research with these groups, but – as in every case – you should reflect if it is justified to 'use' them.

Researchers

Sometimes we find suggestions of 'Just do it' as being the best way of going into the field, finding something new there and developing interesting knowledge from it (e.g. Glaser, 1992, for taking or Punch, 1994, for reviewing such positions). However, we should think about how to prepare our research(ers) carefully for working in the field. To be prepared for contact with people or events in the field, researchers should be trained in using their methodological approach, know what it is about and what problems might arise in applying it. Interview training in role-plays may be helpful, if they are followed by a critical feedback by the research team or the supervisor of a research. Open situations and meeting strangers in order to have a conversation about sensitive topics with them can be a challenge for many researchers, and having some experience with such a setting can be helpful. In particular, if research addresses topics like chronic or terminal illness, contact with interviewees can be not so easy for the researchers, also. Experience with this topic and knowledge about this may obstruct a naïve position, from which researchers see what members in the field do not see any more, but it can also be helpful for getting along with the issue, the participants and the field in general. It can also be a good starting point for developing an ethically sound relationship with the interviewees or participants in the study.

These three angles – relevance, participants, researchers – will not only be issues of an examination by an institutional review board but should be taken into consideration by the researchers in planning the concrete study.

Research questions

There are several ethical issues linked to the formulation of research questions.

Focus of research questions

A central issue here is how focused the question is – does it give a clear advice for what is necessary as data to collect for answering it or not? Unfocused research questions not only make the project more difficult to manage, but also extend the scope of the data to be collected more than necessary. Qualitative research is often understood as open and holistic, and focus accordingly should be developed and refined in the later stage of the project. The consequence of such an approach for the participants is that their life or situation is recorded or talked about more extensively in the research than would be necessary. Thus, the focus of the research question and a clear planning at this stage can prevent participants from being 'over-researched', meaning that they are asked for more insight into their privacy than necessary.

Confrontation through research issues

A second issue in this context to reflect is what the research question might mean for possible research participants. What will they be confronted with when they agree to take part in the research and to answer the questions in the interview? For example, doing interviews with people suffering from a beginning dementia can be very painful for the participants as they are confronted with their forgetfulness and with the gaps in their knowledge, memory or language use. In our homeless project, it can be confrontational to ask the adolescents how their street life began, as this will in most cases lead back to more or less severe conflicts in their family, for example. This confrontation can be necessary for pursuing the goal of the research, and if it is really justified and cannot be avoided, then you should accept it but take precautions to avoid harm to the participants.

Deception in research

A third issue in this stage is linked to the topic of deception in research. It may be a consensus now, that we should not deceive our participants about our research. But at the same time, will it be helpful for the research if we inform our research participants in great detail about our research question? Of course we should inform them about our topic of research, but if we present our research question in detail (for example, including our assumptions of group comparison), we might produce specific expectations or irritations. If we take this into account, the general rule 'No deception!' becomes more difficult on the level of the details of how to put that into concrete terms.

Again, we have identified three angles for assessing ethical issues at this stage of the research. This does not mean that we should not do research, but we should reflect whether how we deal with these issues is justified by the research we pursue.

Access and sampling

Ethics become practically relevant once you approach people for participating in your research, which means once you enter the field of your research.

Informed consent

In approaching the field and our participants, we should prepare a form that regulates the informed consent – wherever this is possible. The best way is to prepare a mutual contract, which explains the purpose of the research, the expectations from the participant (e.g. to give an interview), the procedure with the data (how long it is to be stored, who will have access, how is anonymity guaranteed). This should be signed by both the researcher and the participant and should include a possibility of withdrawing consent. To give the researcher a working basis, a time for withdrawing a signature should be defined (e.g. two weeks). If this can be realized, this contract should also include whether the participant will be given the results or not.

Vulnerable people

In the standard situation, every participant should sign such a contract beforehand. However, there are several exceptions to such a rule. First, experience shows that there are many people who are ready to participate in the research but refuse to sign a document like this. Sometimes we work with people who are not in a situation to sign a contract – such as children, very old people or patients. In such cases, we should clearly define how the informed consent can be guaranteed as a principle, and what kind of substitute could be acceptable. In the first case, the researchers should sign that they informed the participant and that he or she agreed on this basis to take part. In the other cases, we should think about who else can give an informed consent for the participant and if that is justifiable.

No harm

When you approach people to become participants in your research, it should be certain that they do not suffer any disadvantages, harm or risks from taking part. That will be beyond doubt on a general level, but if it comes to details this may become problematic. For example, if you do a study with people in underprivileged conditions of living – say homelessness – you are mostly interested in people in these conditions and not so much in people in general. Therefore, you look for such people and you are somehow reliant on their remaining in such a situation long enough for you to do your interview with them, for example. Of course, there are many projects of action research that intend to change the situation of their participants through the research, but here as well the existence of social problems as a ground for doing the research part is constitutive as well.

Selection

If you do your research in an institution and have to sample interview partners from a group of people who know or are in touch with each other, it can be irritating for the individual not being chosen for participation (am I not interesting enough?) or to see that others are not integrated in the research (why me?). The researchers should reflect such a dynamic they might produce in the field with their sampling decisions.

Collecting data

While collecting data, we should be aware of our influence on the field or on the subjects of our research – not so much in the sense of a bias undermining the quality of our results but seen from the perspective of our partners.

Disturbance

The first is the disturbance we produce with our research – for professional or private routines by standing in the way, by focusing on things otherwise unnoticed by the members of the field, by asking questions or by reactivating memories when asking for family photos, for example. This disturbance can be productive for our research and the knowledge we can produce with it, but it often is an irritation for those who let us into their private or professional lives. Again, this does mean either that we should not do our research for this reason or that we could avoid such a disturbance completely. But we should reflect our impact on the daily life of our participants and should try to limit it to what is absolutely or really necessary.

Being pushy

Research is a dialogue, and not only in interviews, where this may be obvious. This dialogue consists of asking for access (to spaces and observable processes) and information (answers, stories, images, documents, etc.), which are offered in return. Research is often not satisfied by first answers and offers and comes with second questions and probing. In interviews, it is important to develop a feeling for the limits of our participants, when it comes to issues they cannot or do not want to talk about, and for when we should stop insisting. Again, this depends very much on the concrete case and can hardly be decided beforehand or formulated in a general rule. But here we may come to borders of privacy and intimacy we have to respect.

Being ignorant

On the other hand, participants sometimes offer aspects we did not foresee, which might be important for them to talk about or relevant in the context of the issue. Here again, researchers need to develop a sensibility for when to take up such issues to avoid being ignorant of such aspects and to the participant. In this context it is again the balance between working with the participant in a very focused way and taking him or her seriously in what they reflect about the issue beyond what we expected.

Data collection is the part of your research where you come closest to your participants, so that ethics in relation to field and participants become concrete and practical at this stage.

Analyzing data

Being accurate

Analyze your data carefully, read and reread them continuously. Do your analysis systematically by using a method (like theoretical coding for example). Use explicit comparison (among events or among people) rather than implicit comparison based on your assumptions.

Being fair

Try to avoid interpretations of data that come along with a devaluation of people. Be careful not to see people as a result of unconscious forces or drives. Try to respect people's intentions and agencies when you interpret the practices or statements you collected as data. Try to be neutral in conflicts becoming visible in the data, especially if several of your participants are involved. Do not read anything into practices and statements that is not 100 per cent supported by the data. Do not be too fast with (over-) generalizations and try to keep the deviant cases in mind when developing patterns, types and other forms of generalizations. Be careful with internal generalization – when you infer from occasional statements to regular habits or traits of people or institutions, for example.

Being confidential

A major issue in analyzing the data is how to keep the anonymity and privacy of your research participants. Field notes and transcripts should not include concrete information about real persons and sites, but should be anonymized right away. You should avoid talking in your research team about 'real' persons (by using their real names) but talk about cases with anonymous or changed names (aliases). The same applies to sites and institutions. If you do your research in an institution with several interviewees knowing each other in real life, you should be extremely careful how to protect your single interviewees from being identified by their colleagues.

Avoid cemeteries of data

Do not keep your data for the rest of your life, but keep them safely stored as long as you really need them. If your contract with the participant includes that you discard the data after a certain time, do so. If you store them, keep them safely locked and distant from any file that allows identifying the participants in real life. Do not collect and store more data than you need for answering your research question.

These suggestions show the need to be rigorous in analyzing the data and in preventing participants from being identified and the data from being misused by other people than those by whom they were originally given for their research.

Writing, generalization and feedback

In writing, the issues of ethics come up again in a nutshell. Here, it is most important to maintain the anonymity of the participants, of the site and of the institutions in which you collected your data. The history of qualitative research is full of examples where participants in a study found themselves presented in such a way that they or their community were easy to identify (see Punch, 1994, for examples). Here, issues of fairness towards the participants and of keeping a position of fairness among them are most crucial. In writing you should select your wording with respect – to the single participants if you quote them or write about them. Here you have to reflect diversity in the way you formulate. Avoid language that is biased against persons (e.g. because of ethnic group membership or age, etc.) and be sensitive in the use of labels. Reproduce your findings accurately and do not try to modify them (slightly) to meet audiences' expectations. Try to give a transparent account of how you proceeded and arrived at your conclusions. Be careful in your generalizations (see above) and also in the formulations you use. If you want to come back to your participants with your results, plan this step carefully. Find a level of presentation (and of differentiation) that is adequate to your audience. Just giving a scientific presentation of typologies can be confusing; confronting participants with interpretations that go beyond the way of thinking they are used to may be irritating and painful. So plan your feedback procedure carefully!

Key points

- Ethics in qualitative research is not only a general, more abstract issue that can be regulated in codes (although this is an important contribution, too).
- Ethical issues in designing qualitative research arise in the several steps that are addressed by design issues and in all the stages of the research process.
- A major part of research ethics consists of the ethical dilemmas researchers face in the contact with the field and the concrete persons in it and in handling the data.
- Beyond immediate field relations, it is the ways in which data are analyzed, presented and perhaps fed back to the field that make a project ethically sound.

Further reading

The following articles go into more details of ethical issues in qualitative research, as will the other books in *The SAGE Qualitative Research Kit* do for each methodological approach:

Christian, C.G. (2005) 'Ethics and politics in qualitative research', in N. Denzin and Y.S. Lincoln (eds), *The SAGE Handbook of Qualitative Research* (3rd ed.). Thousand Oaks, CA: Sage, pp. 139–64.

Flick, U. (2006) *An Introduction to Qualitative Research* (3rd ed.). London: Sage (chap. 4).

Hopf, C. (2004) 'Research ethics and qualitative research: an overview', in U. Flick, E. von. Kardorff and I. Steinke (eds), *A Companion to Qualitative Research*. London: Sage, pp. 334–9.

Punch, M. (1994) 'Politics and ethics in qualitative research', in N. Denzin and Y.S. Lincoln (eds), *Handbook of Qualitative Research*. Thousand Oaks, CA: Sage, pp. 83–97.

8
Verbal Data

Chapter Objectives
After reading this chapter, you should

- have a first orientation about the major methods of producing verbal data in qualitative research;
- see the specific issues concerning research designs in using these methods; and
- have some orientation about when to use which of these methods in qualitative research.

Introduction

In this and the following chapters, some of the most important qualitative research methods will be briefly presented. The aim is not so much to give a basic introduction to qualitative research or for example interviewing, which could replace an introductory textbook. For such an introduction, you will be referred to the other books of *The SAGE Qualitative Research Kit* (for a more comprehensive introduction from a comparative perspective, see Flick, 2006). Here, the focus will be more on design issues. The aim of the chapter is to relate the issues of constructing research designs to the single methods and thus give an orientation for the other books in *The SAGE Qualitative Research Kit* (Angrosino, 2007; Banks, 2007; Barbour, 2007; Gibbs, 2007; Kvale, 2007; Rapley, 2007).

In general, we can summarize four basic methodological approaches in collecting or producing qualitative data, if we take the sorts of data each approach produces as points of reference:

- The first one is mainly focused on eliciting verbal data – in interviews, in stimulating narratives and in focus groups. Data to be analyzed here are mostly transcripts of recorded interviews or focus groups.
- The second approach is mainly focused on producing descriptions of what has been observed in ethnography or in an (in most cases participant) observation. Data to be analyzed here are mostly more or less extended field notes, memos and the like.
- The third approach is mainly based on transforming documents into (qualitative) social science data – texts, files, photos, films and the like. In some cases, such documents are produced in and for the research; in many cases, existing documents are used. Data to be analyzed then are a corpus of texts, sometimes of visual materials.
- And finally, we find approaches that are based on analyzing the materials produced by one of the other three approaches. These materials can then be analyzed with a more coding-oriented or more narrative or discourse/conversation analytic perspective.

In this and the next three chapters, we will first address the single methods of data collection along the major design issues mentioned in the preceding chapters – like research perspective and questions, sampling, comparison, generalization, triangulation, quality and writing, resources, stepping-stones, basic designs and ethics – and briefly mention an example for its use before we again take a comparative perspective on the different methods in Chapter 11.

Interviews

Interviews are one of the dominant methods in qualitative research. We find different ways of doing an interview (see Kvale, 2007, or Rubin and Rubin, 1995, for more detailed introductions and overviews). In most cases, we find single interviews based on an interview guide, which includes the topics to be addressed in this situation. Normally, interviews are limited to meeting the participant once, after asking the potential interviewee in a preliminary contact (by telephone or face to face) to take part in the study and arranging a meeting for the interview. In some cases, we find repeated interviews (in longitudinal studies); in other cases, we find that researchers come back to the participants to check with them the results of the study.

Beyond this classic form of interview (one face-to-face meeting, one interviewee, a set of questions answered in a more or less open dialogue), we also find special forms of interviews. One is to do a group interview with a number of people at the same time, but based on questions to be answered (different from a focus group). There is also an extended literature about doing narrative interviews – which means asking the interviewees to tell a story (of their lives, or of their illness and the like) instead of expecting them to answer questions. We also find combinations of these approaches – interviews with narrative parts and question–answer parts (for the episodic interview see Flick, 2007). More recently, interviews are sometimes done by using media of communication for interviewing people at distant places as in telephone interviews and Internet interviewing, although these forms are often based on a standardized format of questions (but see qualitative examples in Flick, 2006, chap. 20). There are also more specialized forms of interviews – ethnographic interviews as part of observations or expert interviews defined by the special target group to be interviewed. In most cases, interviews are recorded and transcribed for analysis.

In terms of research design, Rubin and Rubin (1995) suggest a flexible, iterative and continuous design rather than to lay down a plan in the beginning, which is then just executed. Flexible design means that you adapt your selection of interviewees and maybe even some of the questions to the progress of the study and to what you find as accessible and interesting in the field. Iterative design means that you change the sampling plan and the focus of the single interview several times and in several stages, for example by narrowing the focus (of the sampling and/or the questions). Continuous design means to redesign – to adapt and improve the design – throughout the research process. They even suggest including new questions or topics in later interviews.

Research perspective and theory

The focus of interview research is (mostly) the individual experience of the participant, which is seen as relevant for understanding the experience of people in a similar situation. A personal narrative of a cancer patient is collected and analyzed as an example of living with cancer. As Kvale (2007) shows, the situation of the interview is often seen as a construction site of knowledge. In interviews, we do not simply find a reproduction or representation of existing knowledge (which can be judged for its truth), but an interaction about an issue that is part of the knowledge produced in this situation.

The theoretical background of most studies using interviews is to some extent in the tradition of symbolic interactionism – that people reflect about their life and that this form of meaning-making can be accessed as a way of understanding the issues of this reflection. For understanding chronic illness better, it is a fruitful way of asking people about their experience with and reflections about being ill and then comparing these reflections in order to develop a theory, for example.

Research questions

In interviews, we can address questions about personal experiences and meaning-making of personal or more general issues (social problems, political changes, historical events for example). We can address the 'what' and the 'how' in interviews (what is chronic illness for the interviewees, how do they live with their illness, etc.). In narrative (parts of) interviews we can ask for how something has begun, **79** developed or changed, but we cannot address the 'why' or attitudes towards something. This has to be addressed in focused questions. In interviews, we cannot directly access processes of interaction or practices – as in observation – but we can receive versions of and reports by one of the participants, the interviewee.

Sampling

For interviews, sampling is oriented to finding the right people – those who have made the experience relevant for the study. Sampling in most cases is purposeful; random or formal sampling is rather the exception. The interviewees also should be able to reflect about their experience, to verbalize this reflection and be ready to spend some of their time being interviewed. In interview studies, the single participant is seen as the case, but often we look for groups of cases too – for example, a number of people with a specific illness experience. Often, sampling is oriented on specific criteria (like gender, age, profession, etc.), but we also find more iterative ways of sampling. Rubin and Rubin (1995, chap. 4) outline several stages of selecting the interviewees from finding knowledgeable people in the beginning to searching for different points of views (by selecting different kinds of people) and looking for specific cases and people for extending the results and their coverage. Sampling for interview studies in most cases is about finding a variety of cases and experiences and sometimes about finding similar cases for comparison.

As Kvale (2007) underlines, sampling in interviewing not only refers to finding and selecting people to interview but also to finding the right parts in the material. This is sometimes relevant for deciding about transcription and even more for analyzing and understanding the content of the interviews as a whole.

Comparison

In a study using interviews, comparison can start from different levels again. We can compare the interviewees with each other – for example, the illness narratives of several people as cases. Then we can set up a typology of successful and failing ways of coping with an illness. We can also do a more group-oriented comparison – like comparing male and female ways of coping with that experience or problem. More often, comparison of interviews starts on a lower level by comparing the answers of different interviewees to a specific question or parts of narratives by different participants. These comparisons then can be linked back to other features that distinguish subgroups in the sample – gender or age, for example. Another form of comparison in interviews is comparison inside a case: what is the interviewee's definition of health and what do they tell about how they deal with health issues in their daily lives? Then answers to several questions or answers and narratives by the same interviewee are compared.

Generalization

From interviews we can expect several forms of generalization. The first is internal generalization – that we can assume to some extent that the statements in the interview situation can be generalized to what the interviewee thinks and says in other situations also. Depending on the method of sampling that was used, we can also try to generalize our findings to people in a similar situation to that of our interviewees. Kvale (2007) distinguishes here between statistical generalization (which is not very common and feasible for interview studies with small numbers and purposeful sampling) and analytic generalization. In the latter, judgements are made as to how far we can draw conclusions from interviews to other people or other situations. For generalizing from interview results, Rubin and Rubin (1995, pp. 71–6) suggest choosing other interviewees who can extend the scope of the results, orienting on the principle of completeness and testing the results for similarity and dissimilarity until you have reached saturation, which means that more interviews would not add any new insights or perspectives.

Triangulation

Although interviews are used as a stand-alone method in most cases, we find different forms of triangulation here. Interviewing is the method in qualitative research that is most often combined with quantitative research like surveys (see Flick, 2007, for examples). We also find triangulation of interviews with other qualitative approaches like ethnography (where interviewing becomes a part of the 'master' strategy of ethnography) or with methods like participant observation or focus groups. We also find within-methods triangulation in interviews, for example of narratives and question and answer parts (as in the episodic interview).

Quality

A quite extensive discussion of quality issues around interviewing can be found in Kvale (2007). In interview studies, approaches like communicative validation or member checks are used relatively often, as we can come back with the interviewee's statements to be checked by him or her. A tension in this context is how far the interviewers manage to keep the balance between standardization and openness and how flexible they are in using the interview schedule. Here you have to find a balance between collecting similar information from every interviewee (with respect to comparison and analysis) and meeting the needs and situation of the single interviewee. An essential issue here is when and how to probe, to go into more depth or bring in topics the interviewee has so far rather avoided.

Writing

Writing in ethnography also has the function of documenting (and making plausible) that the researcher 'was there' and of giving the reader the impression of knowing what it means to 'be there', and thus is very much focused on context and descriptions. In interview studies, the issue of writing is to give the reader information about what the interviewee(s) said with respect to the issue of the study. A major issue here is the selection of the material to be presented, as it over-challenges most readers to read whole interviews or too lengthy excerpts of interviews. Kvale (2007) underlines that researchers should keep their audience in mind when writing about their research. He sees as problems how to contextualize quotes that are presented, how to keep them readable and make them authentic at the same time. Rubin and Rubin (1995) address similar issues, but stress that reporting from interview studies needs to give an impression of the interviewees' life worlds and that a major concern in writing is how to make the research credible – how to demonstrate that the conclusions drawn from the interviews are grounded in the material and that they are more appropriate than other conclusions.

Basic design

Interviewing can be embedded in different basic designs. We find many retrospective studies using interviews – like life histories or narratives – either as case studies or in a comparative design (see Kvale, 2007, for examples). Interviews can also be embedded in a longitudinal design, as we can come back to the interviewees after some time and ask them similar (or even the same) questions again.

Resources and stepping-stones

For conducting an interview study, several resources are necessary or at least helpful. You should bring expertise with interviewing to the study or develop expertise among the members of the research team. This expertise should cover how to apply the interview guide and questions, how and when to probe, how and when to introduce new topics and the like. For this purpose, interview training could be helpful (role-plays of interviewer and one researcher playing the interviewee with the 'real' questions, videotaping of this role-play and analysis of the tape for the interaction, the answers and the possible ways of probing by the whole team). An important resource for interviewing is to have someone experienced with transcription. In planning the study, it is necessary to have resources for this – either (a lot of) time in the research team or money for paying someone outside to do this. In both cases, transcription consumes a considerable part of the resources. To make this step easier and the results better, it is necessary to have good recording equipment available.

Finding the 'right' interviewees is relevant in this context, as in many cases it proved to be surprisingly difficult to access the people the researcher had in mind when planning the study. It is important to allow enough time for this step and for arranging appointments for the actual interviews. However, quite often interviewers find out that the person they are currently interviewing is not the 'right' one, and that there are fewer potential interviewees to approach than expected (see Kvale, 2007, and Rubin and Rubin, 1995, for such practical matters of planning interviews).

Ethics

Here, informed consent should be an obligation in every study. However, sometimes it is difficult to obtain this directly from the participants, in particular if we want to interview children or very old or sick people. In such a case it should be considered who should be asked for this consent instead (see Flick, 2006, chap. 4). A central matter in this context is the relationship to the interviewee we need to build up. Rubin and Rubin (1995) talk of a conversational partnership in this context. The problem here is how to get in a relation to the interviewee that is close enough for both to be able to talk about sensitive or sometimes embarrassing issues and at the same time for the researchers to avoid false expectations on the part of the interviewee. For both sides, it should be clear that the relation is a specific one (research and not therapy or friendship or the like), without giving the interviewee the feeling of being 'ripped off' or 'abused' by the researcher.

Another issue is confidentiality – how does the researcher take care that the anonymity of the interviewee is maintained throughout the research process and in publications (see Kvale, 2007, for more details about ethics and interviewing).

Example

In our project about health concepts of homeless adolescents (Flick and Röhnsch, 2007) we apply the episodic interview with the adolescents (Flick, 2007). Research questions refer to how these adolescents live in the street, how they deal with health issues and which experiences they make in seeking help in the health system. (The sampling in this study has already been described in Chapter 4.) The interviews combine concrete, focused questions (for example, about what health means for the interviewee) and narrative stimuli focusing on specific situations and experiences. For doing the interview, an interview guide was developed and the adolescents are asked for their concepts of health and their experiences of health, health problems and how they deal with them. They are invited to recount situations referring to such experiences. The interview guide includes several topics:

- How interviewees turned to street life.
- Their subjective definitions of health.
- Their current situation (housing, financial problems, eating) and its consequences for health.
- How they handle health problems and risks (drugs, alcohol, sexuality).

After asking the interviewee to recount how he or she began to live on the street, questions in the interviews are, for example: 'What is that for you, health?' or 'How do you see that you are healthy? Can you please tell me a situation which makes that clear to me?' We receive answers such as the following:

> I feel healthy right now. Well, I can decide myself, what I do (...) I simply feel healthy now at this moment. Because I do not feel the pain, and if I feel the pain, even then I feel health. Because I know, that I don't want to die (...). If I thought the whole time about it 'I have to die', I would make myself even sicker than I am anyway.

We take such statements for comparing the cases (the adolescents) with each other in order to develop typologies of experiences (as a way of generalization) and triangulate the interviews with participant observations in a public space, where the interviewees hang out with their (homeless) peers. The questions in the interview guide are points of orientation, but a major issue of quality for these interviews is how to adapt to the individual interviewees to give them space to unfold experiences and to build a relation to the interviewer. Writing about the results is built on presenting the typologies of cases related to topics (like illness experiences and those with the health professionals, for example) in order to show where there are social differentiations in this social field. The basic design of the study is a comparative one focusing on a description of the current state (a snapshot) with some retrospective parts (how street life started and developed for the interviewee). Major stepping-stones are to find adolescents for the interview and to give them a framework for talking openly. Besides issues of anonymity even in cases where interviewees refer to illegal practices, a major ethical concern is how to avoid false expectations on the part of the interviewees beyond giving them some advice on whom to turn to in case of complaints or problems.

Conclusion

Interviews are an elaborate method for working with people as cases from a comparative perspective. They allow triangulations with different methods and in a variety of basic designs. Research questions address personal experiences and we should take care that our interviewees are aware of the (temporal and personal) limits of the relation in the interview.

Focus Groups

Focus groups have become more prominent again in the last two decades. They are used for research issues and for more pragmatic purposes in marketing, for example (see Barbour, 2007, for a detailed overview). Much of the methodological writing about focus groups develops a perspective including several alternatives, among which researchers can decide according to what they intend to find out by using this method. Thus, traditionally one can decide between groups of people who know each other, who have relations among each other outside the focus group situation, or who have never seen each other before and will not do so after the group. More recently, researchers have started to experiment with virtual focus groups, which means participants in a chat room, for example, or otherwise contacted and communicating via the Internet. For traditional uses of focus groups, several issues of planning arise that are different from those in interviews or ethnography.

Research perspective and theory

Barbour (2007) mentions several purposes for which focus groups should not be used, like eliciting narratives or measuring attitudes. They are more adequate if you want to study interaction in a group about a specific issue. The theoretical background of using focus groups is in some cases symbolic interactionism; in other approaches, the practice is more oriented to discourse and conversation analysis (e.g. in Puchta and Potter, 2004; see also Rapley, 2007).

Research questions

In research contexts (different from marketing), focus groups can be used for research questions interested in the interaction of a number of people about an issue. According to Barbour (2007) they can be used for studying sensitive topics and for integrating people who are hard to reach in studies, which is an advantage in surveys, for example.

Sampling

In preparing focus groups, sampling means basically the composition of groups according to the research question and intended comparisons. The latter also should determine how many groups should be included in a study and how big the single group should be. Group features like homogeneity and heterogeneity should also be set up according to the research interest and purpose of the study. As in interviews, it can be helpful to plan several stages of sampling (second-stage sampling: Barbour, 2007) with criteria developed or modified after the first group(s).

Comparison

With focus groups, two ways of comparison are possible. We can compare between different groups – for example, a group of medical doctors with one of nurses discussing the same issue. We can also compare within groups – what were the different opinions becoming visible in the statements of different

85

members of one discussing group? To make each of these forms of comparison most effective, a well-planned composition and selection of the groups and their members is necessary. More complicated is a systematic comparison of individual members across different groups – in analogy to comparison of single interviews. With focus groups, we have to take the group as a unit and as an intermediate factor into account in such a comparison.

Generalization

As a consequence, generalization in a statistical sense of the word is difficult with focus groups. We can apply analytic generalization, which means that we can theoretically think about the range of the statements in the group. We can also apply internal generalization – reflecting how far some findings are typical for the group or for the discussion it had. External generalization depends on how the variety of groups was constructed: the greater the diversity of the groups and in the groups, the stronger the potential for generalization of the results.

Triangulation

Barbour (2007) addresses the use of focus groups in mixed methods designs, especially in combination with single interviews and sometimes following quantitative research. In our own study on professionals' health concepts, we used focus groups as a way of feeding results back and as a second approach for data collection (see below).

Quality

Issues here are the quality of recording the discussion, of transcribing the group's interaction and the moderator's skills in stimulating a good discussion and in keeping it going and focused. The quality of sampling is relevant in providing the necessary variety of groups and members and the appropriate groups (and members) for the issue of the study. Finally, the rigour of interpretation and analysis varies in focus group research and it is crucial to make the process transparent to readers of reports and publications.

Writing

Here it is seen as important to document the context of the group and the process of their discussion when reporting statements and results from focus group research. It is also important that reporting goes beyond stating what was said but builds on a systematic analysis of statements and processes. Many reports treat focus group data like single interview data and quote and analyze focus group statements like interview statements (Wilkinson, 1998), which undervalues the specific qualities of the data and the sometimes bigger effort to produce them (compared to interviewing).

Basic design

Although we find studies based on one focus group (e.g. Crossley, 2003), in most cases focus groups are used for comparative studies. They can be employed for discussing events and experiences in the past in a retrospective study and of course focus groups can be part of a longitudinal design. But in most cases, focus groups are used in a comparative study producing a snapshot (descriptions of current states of opinions about an issue).

Resources and stepping-stones

For a successful study with focus groups, good recording (several microphones, good digital or tape recording, audio or video) and transcription equipment is necessary. Organizing groups can sometimes be time-consuming (if you need specific participants, for example). Drop-outs are difficult to avoid. Transcription and analysis are again very time-consuming. The capabilities of group moderators or facilitators are an important resource and they should be able to stimulate, moderate and maybe cool down discussions.

Ethics

Here, using the method for vulnerable groups (children, patients) needs extra reflection about the impact of taking part in a focus group on the life situation of the participants, which is a general issue to consider in focus groups. It is important to set up a clear and transparent framework of participation – for example, that participants have the chance to withdraw certain statements and that they know what the whole enterprise is about. You should try to reflect why your participants agreed to take part in the group and what the potential dynamics in the group might be or come from. This can be particularly relevant if you have different ethnic populations in your groups, but also in other cases.

Example

In our study on professionals' health concepts, we used focus groups for two purposes in addition to our interviews: we wanted to see how the professionals discuss the issues of our study (health and prevention in their day-to-day practice) and we wanted to receive a feedback to the results from the earlier interviews. Thus we did several focus groups with either nurses or general practitioners. Sampling was based on the sampling for the interview part of the study, as we wanted to have the same participants in both parts. The sample for the focus groups was smaller because some participants did not want to take part in this step or had to cancel shortly before. Generalization was internal and very limited in external ways (according to our intentions). Triangulation referred to the interviews and comparing both steps and their results with each other was a contribution to the quality of the study as a whole. The basic design of the use of focus groups was here a comparative one. Stepping-stones came from the fact that we 'lost' some of our intended sample, due to refusal or practical problems. We rented a laboratory from a market research institute for running and recording the discussions professionally. We presented the results as part of the report of the whole project focusing on what the participants discussed as possible implications of our results for their professional practice. For ethical reasons we decided to do separate discussions with each professional group to avoid professional conflicts or hierarchies having an impact on the group and the participants.

Conclusions

Focus groups are a method for analyzing and comparing how a number of people discuss an issue. Logics of sampling are different from the single interview, as we should keep the composition of the group in mind when selecting the participants. Generalization here is often limited and not always intended to be very extensive. Triangulation can include interviews but also other methodological approaches.

Key points

- Interviews and focus groups are different ways of producing verbal data.
- Both have strengths and limitations for specific research questions and participants.
- They also follow different logics of sampling, comparison and generalization.

Further reading

The following texts will go into more details for the methods outlined here:

Barbour, R. (2007) *Doing Focus Groups* (Book 4 of *The SAGE Qualitative Research Kit*). London: Sage.

Kvale, S. (2007) *Doing Interviews* (Book 2 of *The SAGE Qualitative Research Kit*). London: Sage.

Puchta, C. and Potter, J. (2004) *Focus Group Practice*. London: Sage.

Rubin, H.J. and Rubin, I.S. (1995) *Qualitative Interviewing*. Thousand Oaks, CA: Sage. (2nd ed. 2005.)

9
Ethnographic and visual data

Chapter objectives
After reading this chapter, you should

- have a first overview of the major methods in this area in qualitative research;
- see the specific issues concerning research designs in studies using these methods; and
- have some orientation about when to use which of these methods in qualitative research.

Introduction

The methods discussed in the previous chapter are aimed at stimulating verbal exchange and data based on the spoken word. The advantage of this is that they have a rather clear focus and that they are in most cases limited to meeting the participants once – for an interview or a focus group. Their disadvantage is that they do not give a direct access to processes and practices but provide accounts, reports and narratives about these. A second limitation is that they will not focus on the visual part of social reality. In this chapter, the focus will be extended in both directions. First, observation and ethnography and then approaches to visual material will be briefly discussed under the major design issues mentioned in earlier chapters.

Ethnography and observation

Ethnography is a rather comprehensive and complex research strategy, which was originally based on participation and observation in open fields or institutions.

Many definitions of ethnography highlight the flexible use of several methods in addition to observation over an extended period of being in the field and participating in one way (or role) or the other. More recently we can observe a shift from role-taking, finding access and data collection to issues of writing about what was experienced and found in analyzing a field. Sometimes descriptions of how to perform ethnography are less methodologically formalized than suggestions for other sorts of qualitative research. However, we also find introductions to ethnography and observations that are taking the issues of this book – research design, planning, sampling and the like – seriously for this type of research also (e.g. Angrosino, 2007; Hammersley and Atkinson, 1995). Maybe we should keep in mind what Hammersley and Atkinson note about the possibilities of planning ethnographic research:

> ... the fact that such research cannot be programmed, that its practice is replete with the unexpected, as any reading of the many published research biographies now available will confirm. More than this, all research is a practical activity requiring the exercise of judgment in context; it is not a matter of simply following methodological rules. (1995, p. 23)

Research perspective and theory

As Angrosino (2007) shows in some detail, ethnography can take a number of theoretical perspectives as starting points. In most cases, however, ethnography is interested in analyzing the making of social situations by taking part in the relevant processes and by observing how they unfold. In most cases, nowadays, ethnography is linked to constructionist and post-modern perspectives.

Research questions

Again, ethnography can be used for several purposes – like identifying a research problem in more detail, identifying sites and persons, or for developing (more formalized) methods (Angrosino, 2007). A more specific use of ethnography is to document social processes. Research questions in ethnography should (mainly) address issues and processes in the here and now of the observation. Past processes can be addressed via traces they left in institutions, signs, development of routines and the like, which influence current practices.

Hammersley and Atkinson (1995) prefer the term 'foreshadowed problems', which they borrowed from Malinowski, for describing what in other contexts is understood as a research question and to develop a research problem to be studied in the current project from this.

Sampling

As Angrosino (2007) holds, sampling and sample size depend on the group you study and the resources you have. However, in observation it is sites and situations rather than groups of persons that are the focus of sampling (compared to interviewing and focus groups). At the same time, the four suggestions he makes can be helpful for selecting a site: it should be likely that you can expect to encounter the issue of your study there, if possible the site should be comparable to sites studied in existing research, it should not be too difficult to access, and you should be able to locate yourself in the site without being too much of a burden to it (Angrosino, 2007). While Angrosino uses the term 'sampling' more in the context of interviews as part of ethnography, Hammersley and Atkinson (1995, p. 42) suggest forms of strategic sampling of cases – especially if you want to test or confirm a theory developed previously. These authors are rather sceptical about studying sites and thus about the potential of sampling sites, because 'the ethnographer is rarely in a position to specify the precise nature of the setting required' (1995, p. 37). At the same time, they define a setting (to be sampled) as a 'named context in which phenomena occur that might be studied from any number of angles; a case is those phenomena seen from one particular angle' (1995, p. 41). Therefore, they argue for (strategic) sampling of cases and for sampling in cases along three major dimensions: time, people and context.

Following these two approaches to selecting empirical material, sampling in ethnography is a three-step process:

- The first step is to select a site in which a problem to be studied is likely to be encountered; if possible, several sites to be able to make comparisons.
- Then, in this site, a (strategic) sampling of cases is the second step, which means reducing the view on the site to a perspective of what is the relevance of the site for answering the research question.
- The third step is to sample in the case, which means to look for people and events in the case that are differently located along the time dimension and for different contexts of such events or people acting in the case.

Time- and context-oriented sampling is necessary because the ethnographer cannot observe or participate around the clock and be everywhere at the same time, so that a major step in a successful ethnography is to identify the right moments and contexts for observation. For selecting the right people to observe or to talk to, researchers may use standard demographic features (age, profession, gender, etc.) for a start but then refine the sampling by developing more sensitive 'observer-identified categories' and also 'member-identified categories' (Lofland, 1976, quoted in Hammersley and Atkinson, 1995, p. 50). This distinction refers to categories (of what a relevant person or situation to address might be) that the researchers develop from their experience in the field or take from what members in the field suggest or mention.

Comparison

In ethnography, comparison may refer to different levels, similar to what has been said about sampling. The most complex level is the comparison between different sites (what has been developed as multi-sited ethnography: see Marcus, 1995). The second level is a comparison within a site – different events, situations or contexts are systematically compared from the angle of the research question. The third level refers to people – what are different forms or types of acting in a field related to an issue (relevant for answering the research question). Intended comparison affects the planning of the study – what to select, how to collect the data in a comparable way or in a way that allows comparing them for the relevant question. But then, comparison is the major step in analyzing the data more or less systematically.

Generalization

Ethnographies are often planned and done as case studies – a specific problem or question is studied in a specific context, which can sometimes be a culture or a country. Generalization to other contexts is then often difficult and not necessarily intended. The intention mostly is rather to present a very detailed description of what has been studied. In this context, the distinction made by Maxwell (2005, p. 115) between 'internal' and 'external' generalization becomes particularly relevant. Giving a detailed description of some practices within a case has the at least implicit basis that the described practices are typical for this case or for some aspects in the case – which means they are not just arbitrary events. Giving an example is always based on referring to something broader or more general. Thus, there is an internal generalization within every description (or other form of analytic presentation of data and interpretations) in ethnography, whereas an external generalization (to other cases or to ways of doing this or that practice in general) is not always linked to ethnographic case studies.

Triangulation

In many examples of ethnographic research we find a rather implicit triangulation (see Flick, 2007, chap. 6): observation, interviewing, document analysis and other forms of collecting data are pragmatically and often only more or less systematically combined in the field, responding to the conditions and options in the field. Angrosino (2007) therefore underlines that a good ethnography is the result of triangulation, using multiple data collection techniques.

Quality

Indicators for quality in ethnography are first of all an extended participation of the researchers – which allows saying that they have really been 'there' and long enough to develop a well-founded understanding of the field and the issue under study. Second, a quality criterion for ethnographies is the flexible use of methods – did the researchers use all sorts of methodological approaches to develop a fuller picture of the issue and the field they studied? The third level of quality assessment in ethnography is on the level of writing – do the researchers produce an account of what they searched and found, which is transparent for the readers also in respect of how they found what they report? (see also Lüders, 2004b, for these issues). Angrosino (2007) refers in this context to a more comprehensive list of quality indicators developed by Miles and Huberman (1994) and applies these indicators to ethnography in more detail (see also Flick, 2007, for the quality of qualitative research in general).

Writing

As already mentioned, writing is a central issue for ethnography in answering the questions about the quality of ethnography as well. There is an extended discussion about different forms and styles of reporting ethnographic research (see Clifford and Marcus, 1986, or van Maanen, 1988), which is linked to more fundamental and epistemological issues of representation and reality, authorship and giving voice to the field and its members, and of what is appropriate in this context. More concrete suggestions of how to plan and structure a report about an ethnographic project are given by Angrosino (2007, chap. 7). In this context, he also discusses non-written forms of presenting ethnographic research, such as films, displays or web-based presentations.

Basic design

Ethnography often uses the case study format as a basic design. It is mostly conceived as a description of the current state (of a site or of a problem in a site). Due to the researchers' extended participation, ethnography comes close to a longitudinal study in some respects (the collection of data over time, for example), but often does not in others (the return to the field or participants after a period without research in order to raise the 'same' questions again, for example). We also find ethnographies done as comparative studies, but rather as exceptions. Ethnography in its core – the use of participation and observation – cannot address issues of earlier times directly. As in other approaches, ethnographers can use interviews to study events of the past. Thus the basic design in ethnography is the case study in the form of a process analysis of the presence at the time of research.

Resources and stepping-stones

For a successful ethnography, personal resources like flexibility, adaptability and situational competence are necessary. If flexibility refers to the use of different methods at the same time, the researcher should be experienced in these different methods (which is sometimes quite a challenge). Another very essential resource is the equipment for recording the data – in the most basic way to take field notes, in more elaborate approaches to videotape or audiotape situations of relevance.

One major issue in this context is access to the site under study in different ways. The optimal site for your study may be too far away for your budget, may be too difficult to access (due to language problems), may be difficult to identify as a site (because of its openness and missing boundaries) and the like. Beyond these general issues of accessibility, researchers may face problems of entry to the field – because of not being accepted by its members (or the institution under study), because of problems of locating themselves in the field (finding a role from which to observe, for example) or because of difficulties in building a rapport with (the relevant) members of the field. Another stepping-stone may be that the issue under study is not available for observation (decision-making in telephone calls instead of meetings, for example). Finally, in ethnography, going native and getting deep enough into the field is a permanent tension for research so that the management of distance and the ability to participate and become a member are central – both as a resource and a stepping-stone.

Ethics

In observational research, ethics become particularly relevant in two ways compared to other forms of (qualitative) research. Ethnography often is a less defined research situation than an interview, for example. Thus, researchers have to pay attention to avoiding any form of covert observation, in which the participants do not know that they are the subject of a research project. Thus, keeping up a situation of 'informed consent', in which participants have been informed about, have agreed to and have had the chance of refusing to be part of research about a specific topic, is more difficult here than in interviews, for example. At the same time – and this is the second way – ethnography is more extensive in invading and capturing participants' lives than for example an interview limited to questions and one meeting with the researcher. Therefore, issues of maintaining and respecting the privacy – and the anonymity – of participants are much more difficult to manage in this type of research. This is even more complicated when photos or films are used as formats for presenting and illustrating findings, although it is a general problem in ethnography.

Example

In our project on homeless adolescents and health (see Flick and Röhnsch, 2007), the part of the research questions in this project we pursue with an ethnographic approach is: how do homeless adolescents communicate about health issues, what are their (observable) health-related practices? Are there common styles of dealing with health issues? Can we find patterns of dealing with health problems? The few sites where we can meet this target group in the city of our study determined the sampling. It was defined by several criteria (age, gender, etc.). So we take a comparative perspective in triangulation with interviewing. A major concern in ethics and in writing about the project is how to protect the anonymity of the participants, if things like using drugs become visible. The quality in this research depends on how far we find access to the group under study and how far we are accepted as partners for a conversation or as someone to be there (and thus in the situation of being an observer). Writing in our study includes ethnographic data for describing the context of the statements from the interview and for outlining the context of the situation of our participants.

Conclusion

Ethnography is an approach for studying groups and processes in their natural settings, which needs a flexible use of methods and a lot of patience in and with the field. Data can be less systematic than in other methods but can be more holistic in the descriptions they make possible. Therefore, generalization here is often more internal – in the context – than beyond the sites and fields under study.

Visual methods

Although we find a long tradition of using photos (and later films) in qualitative research – as data or for documenting data – we can observe a renaissance or boom in visual sociology or visual anthropology in the last two decades. Using visual material or giving a camera to participants for recording aspects of their life world (relevant to the research question) is a way of seeing through the eyes of the participants. Basically we find four ways of using visual data. The researchers themselves may produce videos or photos (like or instead of invading field notes) and analyze them, or they may use materials produced by members of the field under study (often materials produced for everyday purposes and not for the research). A more recent sort of data is coming from the Internet – web pages, for example. Finally, we can use for example television series (soap operas) for analyzing how they represent a field or topic.

Research perspective and theory

Banks (2007) refers to several theoretical backgrounds of visual research such as cultural studies, which are rethought from several angles: a more phenomenological one, by taking contexts of images more into account, and by focusing the relation of power and images. We also find approaches interested in the relation of the manifest and the latent in the content of the image and ethnomethodology as a background.

Research questions

In visual research, questions of content and form are addressed: What is the content of an image and how is it constructed or transported? What is the meaning and the message to be transported and how are recipients addressed through this material?

Sampling

Sampling may address different levels: concrete images, which are selected according to one of the suggestions discussed here in Chapter 3; contexts of image production or use for comparing them; producers or users of images who are then compared for their relation to the material with respect to the research question. In TV studies, we would have to select single sequels or episodes from a sequence of broadcasts or from inside the sequel.

Comparison

Again, we can identify different levels of comparison with visual materials: the images, the producers or users, and the contexts in which they are made or used. A fourth level, which can be linked to each of the other three, and most strongly to the first one, is a distinction of comparison for contents, for formal structures and means and for the relation of both: what is the content of several images, which means are used for presenting them in each case and how are both related in the examples?

Generalization

The strength of images is their richness in context and the amount of specific information they transport. This can sometimes make it more difficult to generalize from images and from studies using images. In particular, traditions of ethnographic filming have a strong focus on the cases they study and document. Nevertheless, an analysis of images, which reflects their specific relation to the context they represent, can allow making generalizations, for example by asking how far and in which respects is this image or set of images typical for a specific context.

Triangulation

Images are often used in combination with interviews, sometimes in the context of a more ethnographic approach to a specific life world.

Quality

Banks (2007) highlights two approaches for assessing the quality of research in this context: to ensure the distinctiveness of visual research (for the specific issue of the study) and the robustness of the research, which can be reached by formalizing methodological approaches. However, much of the use of visual methods in qualitative research depends for its quality on the flexibility in approaching and analyzing the materials. Another specific dimension of research quality here is the quality of the materials on the level of making a photo and of reproducing it (the quality of the prints or the display), for example.

Writing

If you want to present visual research appropriately, you will soon be confronted with going beyond the written word. Films can be a medium for presenting research results in themselves, and if you want to use them you will have to find an appropriate way of dealing with anonymity and confidentiality in what you present. A specific problem is how to present images you used in your research, as you may need other media than writing an article, for example. Images need more space than words and they provide more context at the same time. The latter makes anonymization more difficult than in writing.

Basic design

Depending on the approach and the research question, visual methods are used in case studies (ethnographic filming, for example) or in comparative studies (photo-elicitation techniques, in which participants are asked to make some photos and then interviewed about them). Although it is possible to use visual methods in longitudinal studies, they are more often part of a retrospective design or even more of a snapshot design documenting current states and processes.

Resources and stepping-stones

Using visual material means using media of documentation or presentation – like printouts of photos, like CDs or DVDs for storing these materials, or videotapes and the like. Sometimes you need extra copies of these media to give them back to participants. You will also need good cameras and media for displaying visual material, extra-fast computers for working with them and the like. All these aspects become relevant on the level of budgeting your project as extra costs you have to take into account. Viewing and reviewing visual materials can take a lot of time, too, and if you work with them on the basis of transcripts, that can become time-consuming as well.

Ethics

In using visual methods, the same ethical issues arise as in other forms of research – how to be sure that the research is based on informed consent, how to maintain anonymity of the participants, how to be fair to them in analyzing them and their life world and the like. However, there are some particular issues linked to images. First of all, it may be more difficult to maintain the anonymity of participants if you reproduce images of them or their life. This means you have to be more careful about anonymization. If you use images of your participants (their family photos, for example) in publications, issues of permission and copyright might arise. There also may be other people on the images (relatives of your participants), whom you could not ask for permission and consent (for example, because they are no longer alive), but whose rights and interests might be harmed by being part of your research (see Banks, 2007, for more details).

Example

In one of our studies, we were interested in which image of nursing as a profession was produced by a hospital soap in Germany (similar to the US medical drama *ER*). We were interested in whether such a serial was transporting and maybe reinforcing traditional images of nursing as a profession or if it takes into account that the profession is changing (through becoming an academic profession, for example) and how the relation between nursing and medicine was presented in role clichés. Several steps were part of the project. First, the single sequel of the series, which was selected, was viewed several times as a whole and impressions and deepening research questions were noted. The results were several complexes of topics (e.g. collaboration and professional profile of nursing). Then, guiding principles for analyzing the material were formulated: 'nursing as maternal service', 'nursing as auxiliary job' and 'internal and external perception of nursing'. Then fifteen core sequences were analyzed in more detail in a microanalysis including the sequence of activities, mimics, gesture, intonation and paralinguistic features like the position of the actors towards each other, composition of images and focus of the camera. In the end, we looked for more general patterns (see Denzin, 2004). The basic design was a case study (the TV series); we could have used several methods of triangulation (with interviews of audiences), but did not due to limited resources. Presentations were focused on the patterns we found and generalization was more internal.

Conclusion

Visual methods can be very useful for analyzing images, TV or film materials. Necessary time and material resources can be bigger than in other methods. You can rely on different basic designs in visual analyses. Generalization can be internal and sometimes is external depending on the research question and the focus of the analysis. Ethical concerns are about reproducing images of living or dead people in publications in a way that takes their personal interests into account.

Key points

- Ethnography and visual methods will produce richer and more contextualized data.
- They present additional problems for maintaining anonymity and confidentiality for the participants, when you use examples in publications.
- They also demand new and appropriate ways of presenting research and findings.

Further reading

These books will extend the issues briefly outlined here in much more detail:

Angrosino, M. (2007) *Doing Ethnographic and Observational Research* (Book 3 of *The SAGE Qualitative Research Kit*). London: Sage.
Banks, M. (2007) *Using Visual Data in Qualitative Research* (Book 5 of *The SAGE Qualitative Research Kit*) London: Sage.

10
Analyzing qualitative data

Chapter objectives
After reading this chapter, you should

- have a first orientation about the major approaches in analysing qualitative data;
- see the specific issues concerning research designs in using these methods; and
- have some orientation about when to use which methods of analysis in qualitative research.

Introduction

The methods briefly presented in the preceding chapters are focused on collecting data (like interviews or focus groups). Or they consist of a more integrated approach (a link between a specific sort of data and a way of analyzing it – visual data or discourse analysis, for example). In this penultimate chapter, we will turn to approaches in which the analysis of qualitative data is in the foreground. Here we will find two different ways – coding and categorizing, which can be applied to qualitative data in general, whereas later a more specified analysis of data will be presented. At the end of this chapter we will try to bring the different issue of this book – the design issues and the methods – together for some kind of outlook.

Coding and categorizing

Coding and categorizing are ways of analyzing that can be applied to all sorts of data and are not focused on a specific method of data collection. This is not the only way of analyzing data, but it is the most prominent one, if the data result from interviews, focus groups or observations. In particular, if computers are used for analyzing qualitative data, one or the other form of coding will be applied. The main activities are to search for relevant parts of the data and to analyze them by comparing them with other data and by naming and classifying them. Through this process, a structure in the data is developed as a step towards a comprehensive understanding of the issue, the field, and last but not least the data themselves. It is suggested to interlink data collection with their analysis in order to profit from insights from the analysis for the process of collecting further data.

Research perspective and theory

The background of coding and categorizing can be realist or constructivist (Gibbs, 2007). The aim is often to develop a theory and therefore the categories for coding the material are developed from the material rather than from existing theories, although this way is possible and usual as well. The approaches need materials at hand – existing documents, transcriptions of interviews, focus groups or interactions. They can also be applied to visual material or Internet material.

Research questions

These approaches are open to all sorts of research topics. They are less appropriate where formal structures (like organizations of specific forms of talk as in conversation analysis) are the main issue. Although narratives can be analyzed with coding and categories as well (see Gibbs, 2007, chap. 5), an analysis interested in the internal structure and the gestalt of the narrative is more difficult with coding.

Sampling

When this form of analysis starts, sampling of cases and materials is often already completed. However, sampling in qualitative research can and maybe even should be based on the progress of the analysis of the data collected so far. Therefore, this form of analysis can have an impact on the sampling of cases and materials. During the analysis, sampling in the case and in the material is an important element.

Comparison

Here we can plan comparisons on three levels: Within a category – what do we find in different interviews, for example, as relevant for a specific category? **101**

Within a case – what does the interviewee say about different issues, how consistent or contradictory are statements across several categories? Between cases – how different or similar are the responses of various interviewees on the level of one topic/category or on the level of the whole interview? Comparisons on the basis of focus groups or observations can be made on similar levels. Comparison here can be facilitated by ordering and structuring – like building a hierarchy between categories, by developing tables for displaying several cases and categories allowing case-by-case or chronological comparisons (see Gibbs, 2007).

Generalization

Constant comparison of materials is an important step on the way from the single case to more (or less) general statements drawn from analyzing the data. To avoid over-generalization, researchers should carefully reflect the boundaries of their data and the sample of people (or materials) they are based on.

Triangulation

Coding and categorizing can be combined with quantitative analyses of standardized data. It may also refer to different sorts and sources of qualitative data. Also, Gibbs (2007) argues for triangulating the perspectives of different researchers on the data as well as seeking for respondent validation – to integrate participants' perspectives on the data into the final analysis.

Quality

Central for the quality of data analysis, according to Gibbs (2007), is that the researchers are reflexive in their practice with the data by critically assessing their own roles as researchers as well as the data and the findings and conclusions drawn from them. Reliability can be increased by rechecking the transcripts and by cross-checking the codes.

Writing

In this context, writing is not only referring to presenting results in a report to audiences. All sorts of research materials like memos, protocols, field notes and research diaries can become relevant for the analysis and are products of the researchers' writing processes. In reports about the research, a good relation between categories that are presented, analysis and conclusions based on them, and excerpts from the 'raw' material is an important goal.

Basic design

In most cases, coding and categorizing will be based on a comparative design. It can be applied in retrospective or longitudinal design as well as in snapshots, because this is decided more by the sort of data (and their focus and collection) that is used for the study.

Resources and stepping-stones

Analyzing qualitative data in most cases is a time-consuming step in the research, which needs most of the resources of a project. A good transcription will make this step easier to handle, but you will need to spend time or money on this step, if it is to be a good basis for interpretation. Using computers can be helpful for supporting qualitative analysis in two cases in particular: if you are already experienced with the software you want to use and if you have a bigger corpus of data. A major problem to avoid is to have an unclear research question and not to have focused it again when you begin your analysis. Another problem may arise when you find out that your data actually do not include those statements or issues you discover as important for your analysis in later stages.

Ethics

In the analysis of qualitative data, anonymity and confidentiality are central issues from the angle of ethics – in transcription, in analysis itself, and most of all in presenting results and excerpts from the data. For example, researchers should be sure that those who do the transcription keep up standards of confidentiality. If you feed your results back to participants, you should take care that they do not feel embarrassed or hurt by your interpretation, without giving them a chance to reflect with you on what was disturbing them. Interpretations should be fair to the research participants (and maybe the institutions) in the research.

Example

In our project on homeless adolescents, we used thematic coding (Flick, 2006) for data analysis, beginning with all statements referring to an area (e.g. meaning of health) for every interviewee. Comparative dimensions are defined across cases for finding commonalities and differences between the various interviews. Cases are grouped along these dimensions and analyzed for specific combinations of features. Contrasting cases allow comparing the cases in one group for similarities and comparing cases across the groups for existing differences among them. Interpretive and practice patterns can be found and analyzed in this way. Stepping-stones are missing statements by one or more participants about specific issues.

Conclusion

Using codes and categories for analyzing qualitative data is quite flexible in the sort of data to be used and how the study is designed. It is mostly planned with the aim of comparing data and cases. Triangulation should include different researchers working on the same material for extending the perspectives. Presentations should take the relation between original material and categories or dimensions into account so that the analysis becomes transparent.

Analysis of conversations, discourse and documents

In these forms of qualitative analysis, data collection is often limited to selecting material (like documents or newspaper articles) and to documenting everyday routines (like tape-recording a conversation between doctor and patient). Here, research interests often focus more on formal aspects – how is a conversation started, continued and ended, what are the structural aspects of a document like a patient record – than on content. In discourse analysis, the stress is more on content, however, compared to conversation analysis. In discourse analysis we also find the use of interviews, observations and focus groups as sources for materials to analyze.

Research perspective and theory

The theoretical background is in most cases ethnomethodology and discourse theory and the interest is in how communication and practices are constructed in everyday life in concrete circumstances. Therefore, the single actor is less focused than interaction processes. On the epistemological level, these approaches are based on social constructionism and theories of (written or spoken) language use in practical contexts.

Research questions

The primary research question of these kinds of research is: how is a specific issue constructed in some sort of communication and which 'methods' do participants in this communication use for this construction? Thus, documents are always produced by someone and for some audience, for some purpose and by using some communicative devices in order to create a certain format of information. This can be a specific way of communicating with a patient about her illness in a doctor–patient communication, which aims at having a diagnosis, a treatment and a plan for proceeding further at the end of the session. This can also be a record produced about this patient, her history as a patient, diagnosis treatments and prognosis or a public discussion about this specific illness in the newspaper with the purpose of creating a moral discourse about the disease and the people concerned with it. In each case the methods of producing the specific document or result are in the focus of this sort of research.

Sampling

As Rapley (2007) holds, the strategy here is building an archive of materials for analyzing the discourse or documents. Selection or sampling then refers to the documents to choose for this archive. Sampling in this kind of research first aims at constructing a corpus of material, which then can be a starting point for sampling inside the materials in this corpus.

Comparison

In conversation analysis, comparison is in many cases oriented towards a more general model (of how a conversation or a telephone call works), which is juxtaposed to the concrete case that is being studied. Often you will set up an inventory of several exemplars (like a number of beginnings of a counselling conversation) and then compare them with each other to find regular and structural principles in them. Comparison of documents is either focusing the contents or the structure of a series of examples.

Generalization

Discourse analysis is more interested in case studies, so that we can mostly find internal generalization here, whereas conversation analysis in most cases is interested in identifying general principles of talk and conversations. In this aim, a generalization from case studies to comparing different cases to general models is implied.

Triangulation

Rapley (2007) mentions the combination of analyzing documents and conversations in this context. A different way is to combine conversation analysis with interviewing, for example for analyzing professional practices by analyzing conversations and professional knowledge by doing and analyzing interviews (see below).

Quality

In studying conversation, discourse and documents, Rapley (2007) holds that there is no claim about truth in interpretations that can be justified. Rather,

105

researchers should try to convince the reader that their interpretations are plausible and credible by showing how they are based on materials and their analysis. Another approach to quality here is to validate documents in team meetings of the research group. In general it should become visible in the results and their presentations, how the researchers have checked and rechecked their conclusions against the material and especially against cases and materials that are deviant from their findings, conclusions and generalizations (as in a typology: see Flick, 2007, for managing diversity in qualitative analysis).

Writing

Depending on the research questions and the materials used in the study, different forms of writing can be appropriate here. An important issue here is how to demonstrate how conclusions are based in the material, and in particular in conversation analysis with its sometimes very detailed transcriptions, how to present excerpts from the material in an accessible and readable way. Too detailed a transcription can obstruct the perspective on the content and context of what is said; too simplified presentations of transcripts may undermine (the impression of) exactness. In discourse analysis in particular, writing and analysis are very closely linked to each other and writing up has an impact on the analysis (new ideas, categories or clarifications).

Basic design

Most research in these areas is providing a snapshot – analyzing materials in the here and now for what contents it includes or how it is structured. Conversation analysis is mostly based on comparing different examples (of counselling interaction, for example), whereas many discourse analyses are based on case studies. In document analysis we often find a retrospective approach (for example, how has the documentation of diagnoses of mental illness changed over the years?).

Resources and stepping-stones

In conversation analysis a major resource you need is time (and money) for transcription of what has been recorded before (with very good equipment if possible – another necessary resource). Finding and accessing the relevant material for describing the discourse about an issue can be difficult and time- consuming as well. This will be the case, in particular, if you want to have (all) the relevant material and not just a single example or an awkward selection. In conversation and document analysis, a danger is to forget about the contents and their meaning in analyzing basically the structure of the material.

Ethics

If you base your research on (audio or video) recording for producing data, you will have to make sure that the participants know about and have consented to being recorded and that they have the chance to make you stop your recording if necessary. With the material you have to take care of anonymity issues – that nobody is identified in or through your research and that you do not talk openly about your participants. Here again, such issues become more difficult once you work with vulnerable people or sensitive topics (see Rapley, 2007, chap. 3).

Example

In a study in the field of community psychiatry, I could show, for counselling conversations, how starting into conversation is organized so that a consultation begins and not something different. In the conversations analyzed, such a start may be designed rather open-ended (e.g. 'What made you come to us?' or 'And what is it about?' or 'What is your desire?'). In other cases, they name the (given) topic for the counselling, or specific characteristics in the way the counselling conversation came into being. These openings, which begin the actual counselling relationship and delimit it against other forms of talk, are sometimes linked to explanations about the way the conversation came about. These explanations are specific for the situation (e.g. 'So, your brother gave me a call').

In analyses of the ending of first contacts in counselling processes, I could show two tasks to be achieved. A timely ending of the conversation has to be ensured. At the same time, the counsellor has to guarantee the continuation of the relation. This analysis could show which formal steps counselling conversations ran through more or less regularly. It could also show how these steps not only built up the conversation in itself, but also were influential in processing the clients and their cases – regardless of the specific content of their problems. So, the analysis was more formal than content-oriented, but shows the construction of cases in the conversations. Sampling was oriented towards cases of conversation and then to formal parts (beginnings, endings) in it; comparison of these parts was the aim of the design and analysis. Ethical concerns are about having the informed consent of clients and the counsellors and to maintain the privacy of both. This conversation analysis was triangulated with interviewing the counsellor, whose consultation was analyzed.

Conclusion

These analyses often focus formal parts of verbal exchange more than the content, although discourse analysis is interested in both – form and content. Basic designs are comparative snapshots in most cases, although documents are sometimes studied with a retrospective focus. From an ethical point of view, anonymity and the sometimes confrontational character of the analysis should be taken into account, in particular if you use the results (and examples) for training or other practical purposes.

▥ Key points

- These approaches to analyzing qualitative data are either quite open in the theoretical approach (as in coding) or come with a background (ethnomethodology in conversation analysis).
- They stress either content or formal structures.
- In both cases, ethics demand a special care for the anonymity of the participants in the analysis.

Further reading

The following books will go into more detail about the methods outlined in this chapter:

Gibbs, G. R. (2007) *Analyzing Qualitative Data* (Book 6 of *The SAGE Qualitative Research Kit*). London: Sage.

Rapley, T. (2007) *Doing Conversation, Discourse and Document Analysis* (Book 7 of *The SAGE Qualitative Research Kit*). London: Sage.

11
Designing qualitative research: some conclusions

Chapter objectives
After reading this chapter, you should

- be able to locate qualitative methods in basic designs;
- see the specific issues concerning research designs in using these methods;
- have some orientation about the role of research proposals for clarifying research designs (and vice versa); and
- have some guideline about writing a research proposal.

Methods and basic designs

In the last three chapters, we have summarized the issues of designing qualitative research unfolded in the preceding chapters and applied them to the methods that will be outlined in more details in the other books in *The SAGE Qualitative Research Kit*. To bring these issues together, two more steps will follow. First, we locate the different methodological approaches along the two axes that were used before (in Fig. 4.4) to structure the basic designs of qualitative research. In Fig. 11.1, each method is located close to the most typical design in which it is normally used. Some of the methods will appear more than once, which shows that some of them are more flexible for being used in different designs, whereas others are more closely linked to one basic design. So you will find ethnography located between snapshots and a longitudinal study both with a case study or comparative perspective. Interviews can be used in almost every

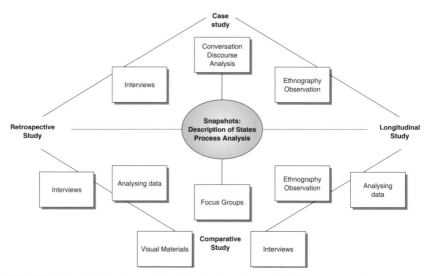

FIGURE 11.1   Methods and basic designs in qualitative research

form or combination of basic designs, as well as approaches to analyzing data. Discourse analysis is more often linked to a case study design, whereas focus groups mostly are used for snapshots in a comparative perspective.

This figure gives you a rough orientation of the link between method and design in one direction. The other direction is to summarize the most important design issues for each of the methods that were outlined in this book and *The SAGE Qualitative Research Kit*.

Design issues in qualitative methods

In Table 11.1 the design issues briefly discussed in the last three chapters are summarized again for each method. Here you will find the most important or most difficult issues mentioned.

Making design issues explicit: Proposal writing

In this book, a number of relevant issues for constructing a research design have been outlined. Other books on this topic have linked research design very closely to writing a proposal, and have sometimes seen it as the same (e.g. Creswell, 2003). Here, designing qualitative research is seen as an internal need of any sort of qualitative research (even if the concreteness and the degree of structure and formalization may vary from approach to approach). It is not understood as just

TABLE 11.1 Qualitative methods and design issues

Design issue	Interviews	Focus groups	Ethnography	Visual methods	Coding and categorizing data	Conversation and discourse analysis
Research perspective Theory	Subjective viewpoints Symbolic interaction	Interaction in groups about a topic Symbolic interaction, discourse	Description of social situations Post-modernism, constructivism	Content and structure of images Cultural studies, ethnomethodology	Theory development Realism, constructivism	Communication in the making Ethnomethodology, discourse
Research questions	Personal experiences and meaning	Sensitive topics	Social processes, foreshadowed problems	Form, content and meaning of images	All sorts of content, not so much structures	Forms and methods of communication
Sampling	Persons as cases	Groups and participants	Sites, cases, within cases	Images, producers	In the material	Building an archive of material
Comparison	Cases or dimensions	Between and in groups	Sites, within sites, people	Audiences, contexts of use	Within and between categories, cases	Inventory for developing a model
Generalization	Internal or analytic to other people	Internal or analytic	Internal or analytic	Internal due to context link	Constant comparison, boundaries of data or sample	Case studies or general principles
Triangulation	Observation, focus groups, surveys	Mixed methods, interviews,	Implicit, using interviews and documents	Interviews, ethnography	Different researchers	Documents, interviews
Quality	Probing and member checks	Moderation, recording, transcription	Extended participation, flexibility	Distinctiveness, robustness, quality of materials	Reflexivity, reliability, cross-checks	Credibility validation in teams, deviant cases
Writing	Relation of conclusions and raw material	Context of the group for participants' statements	Transparency of the field; media other than text	Visual presentations; media other than text	Relation of categories and data in presentation	Accessible presentation of examples

(Continued)

TABLE 11.1 (Continued)

Design issue	Interviews	Focus groups	Ethnography	Visual methods	Coding and categorizing data	Conversation and discourse analysis
Basic design	Comparative, retrospective	Comparative, snapshot	Case study	Case study	Comparative design	Snapshot, comparative
Resources	Experience with interviewing, transcription	Recording equipment	Getting there, documentation	Technical media, time for (re-)viewing materials	Transcriptions, computers and software expertise	Recording and transcription
Stepping-stones	Finding the 'right' cases	Having the 'right' participants in the group, drop-outs	Accessing 'invisible' phenomena	Adequate ways of displaying materials	Missing data, unclear focus	Relation of form and content
Ethics	Informed consent, confidentiality, relation to interviewee	Vulnerable people, group dynamics	Informed consent, anonymity	Anonymity of (other) persons on images, rich context	Confidentiality, anonymity, if feedback to members: fairness	Informed consent, anonymity
Further reading	Kvale (2007)	Barbour (2007)	Angrosino (2007)	Banks (2007)	Gibbs (2007)	Rapley (2007)

TABLE 11.2 Model for a proposal structure

---

1 Introduction
2 Research problem
   (a) Existing literature
   (b) Gaps in the existing research
   (c) Research interest
3 Purpose of the study
4 Research questions
5 Methods and procedures
   (a) Characteristics of qualitative research and why it is appropriate here
   (b) Research strategy
   (c) Research design
      (i) Sampling
      (ii) Comparison
      (iii) Expected number of participants/cases/sites/documents
   (d) Methods of data collection
   (e) Methods of data analysis
   (f) Quality issues
6 Ethical issues
7 Expected results
8 Significance, relevance, practical implications of the study
9 Preliminary pilot findings, earlier research, experience of the researcher(s)
10 Timeline, proposed budget
11 References

---

something outward bound – relevant if you go out with your research to apply for some funding or permission from an institutional review board or from a PhD commission. In any context, however, writing a proposal can be very helpful for reflecting your design and for making it explicit. Therefore, I want to end this brief overview of design issues in qualitative research with some suggestions for how to turn them into a research proposal.

There is no commonly accepted structure or format for a research proposal. Sometimes, funding agencies or institutional boards have set up a model structure, or experience from earlier application shows that they expect a specific structure. Then you should of course try to meet these expectations. As a general structure for a proposal we can suggest the following model (see Table 11.2).

Designing the research becomes relevant in this context in two respects: first as an extra point in the structure suggested in Table 11.2; second as a perspective on the soundness of the whole project. Do the research problem, questions, methods, resources, proposed funding, timeline and ethics fit together into a sound outline, plan and proposal?

For making the research (and beforehand the proposal) work, there are some guidelines to keep in mind:

- You should try to make the design of your research and the methods as explicit and clear in as much detail as possible.
- Research questions and the relevance of planned procedures and expected data and results for answering them should be explicit and clear in as much detail as possible.
- The study and the expected results and implication should be put into academic and practical context.
- Ethics and procedures should be reflected as far as possible.
- Methods should not only be made explicit in the how (of their use) but also in the why (of their selection).
- Plans, timelines, existing experiences and competences, methods and resources should fit into a sound program for your research and be made explicit in this way.

If you take these guidelines into account and know enough about the area and problem you want to study, your proposal should be accepted and your research should work, although there are always circumstances, problems and stepping-stones that might arise for both. More information about the methods you choose, or the range of methods you might choose your method from, can be found in the other books of *The SAGE Qualitative Research Kit*.

Key points

- A (good) research design is relevant for doing research successfully, not only for successfully writing a proposal.
- Nevertheless, writing a proposal can be helpful for examining the soundness of your research design and a basis on which others (reviewers for example) can do such an examination.
- Methods can be allocated in different ways to basic designs in qualitative research.
- Design issues apply in different ways to different methods.

Further reading

These books will complement this book in their perspective on research design. The other books in *The SAGE Qualitative Research Kit* will go into more detail for the single method or approach:

Marshall, C. and Rossman, G.B. (2006) *Designing Qualitative Research* (4th ed.). Thousand Oaks, CA: Sage.
Maxwell, J.A. (2005) *Qualitative Research Design – An Interactive Approach* (2nd ed.). Thousand Oaks, CA: Sage.

III Glossary

Action research An approach in which research has the major function to change the site under study and to activate and enable the participants to initiate changes.

Appropriateness Methods should fit the issues under study and thus the issues become the point of reference.

Audiences People or institutions you write for and want to address, when you report or publish your research.

Audiencing Writing a text with the special readership and its expectation in mind.

Background theories Theories that are informing qualitative research approaches with a specific concept of reality and research.

Basic design There are a number of designs that are very typical or used very often in qualitative research and represent a number of different types of research (e.g. case study or longitudinal study).

Categorizing To allocate pieces of data with other pieces to one term or headline in order to materialize their similarity or to different terms in order to materialize their distinctiveness.

Chicago School A very influential group of researchers and approaches in the history of qualitative research at the University of Chicago, the background of approaches like grounded theory.

Code of ethnics Professional associations set up rules of good practice in research (or interventions) as an orientation for their members.

Coding To label pieces of data and allocate other pieces of data to them (and the label). Development of concepts in the context of grounded theory.

Communicative validation Assessment of results (or of data) by asking the participants for their consensus.

Constructionism A variety of epistemologies in which the social reality is seen as the result of constructive processes (activities of the members or processes in their minds).

Continuous design Approaches to research design that emphasize the ongoing development of the design throughout the research process.

Conversation analysis Study of language (use) for formal aspects (how is a conversation started or ended, how are turns from one speaker to the other organized).

Corpus A set of materials or data for analyzing it (e.g. a corpus of newspaper texts for a discourse analysis).

Credibility Criterion for evaluating qualitative research based on prolonged engagement in the field.

Deception of research participants Giving participants wrong information about the aims of the research or their role in it.

Discourse analysis Studies of how language is used in certain contexts, for example how specific identities, practices, knowledge or meanings are produced by describing something in just that way compared to other ways.

Dissemination Publishing results or reporting them back to participants or fields under study.

Episodic interview This interview combines question/answer sequences with narratives (of episodes).

Epistemology Theories of knowledge and perception in science.

Ethnography Research strategy combining different methods, but based on participation, observation and writing about a field under study.

Ethnomethodology Theoretical approach interested in analyzing the methods people use in their everyday life to make communication and routines work.

Evaluation Use of research methods for estimating and deciding about the success of an intervention.

Extended participation Staying long enough in a field under study to understand processes and routines in this field. Used as a quality criterion in ethnography.

External generalization Transfer of results beyond the people, fields, etc., that were studied.

Flexible design Approach to adapt research designs to the concrete field and the development of the project.

Focus group A group that is invited to discuss the issue of a study for research purposes.

Foreshadowed problems Sometimes used in ethnography instead of formulating a research question. What will the researchers identify and study as a problem in the field?

Formative theory A more general theory (in grounded theory research) referring to more than one area.

Gatekeepers People regulating formally or informally the access to a research field (or to the medical system, for example).

Generalization Transfer of research results to situations and populations that were not part of the research situation.

Grounded theory Theories developed from analyzing empirical material or from studying a field or process.

Indication Decision about when exactly (under which conditions) a specific method (or combination of methods) should be used.

Informed consent Participants in a study are informed that they are studied and given the chance to say no to the research.

Inquiry Another word for research.

Institutional review boards A committee that reviews research proposals for how far they meet ethical guidelines and standards.

Internal generalization Transfer of findings or interpretations to the cases under study as a whole.

Interview training Role-play for simulating an interview in a group of observers and analyzing it afterwards for the interviewer's non-verbal behaviour, use of questions, relation to the interviewee and mistakes in general.

Iterative design Approach to finalize a research design step by step according to the experiences in the field.

Longitudinal studies A design in which the researchers come back repeatedly after some time to the field and the participants to do interviews several times again in order to analyze development and changes.

Member check Assessment of results (or of data) by asking the participants for their consensus.

Milgram experiment An experiment in which people were brought in a (simulated) situation where they hurt other people following instructions of an experimenter.

Mixed methodologies An approach of combining qualitative and quantitative methods on a rather pragmatic level.

Multi-sited ethnography Here, ethnography is applied to several fields aiming at comparing these fields.

Narrative interview Participants are asked to tell the story of their lives (or their illness, for example) as a whole, without being interrupted with questions by the interviewer.

Naturalistic approach Research going into the life world of people to study them in their 'natural' contexts.

Negative case Case (or more generally, empirical material) not fitting in or supporting a model or other forms of findings.

New public health Orientation in the health system towards prevention and social circumstances of illness.

Objectivity The degree to which a research situation (the application of methods and their outcome) is independent from the single researcher.

Operating costs Refers to the costs you need on a very basic level when you do a qualitative project (technical equipment, consumption of materials, etc.).

Paradigmatic core of qualitative research Common features of different approaches and research programs summarized under the label 'qualitative research'.

Participant observation The researcher becomes a member of the field under study in order to do observation.

Participatory research The people who are studied are not only 'objects' of research, but are actively involved in doing and perhaps planning the research.

Phenomenology Careful description and analyses of consciousness, with a focus on the subjects' life world.

Positivism A philosophy of science that bases the latter on the observation of data. The observation of data should be separated from the interpretation of their meanings. Truth is to be found by following general rules of method, largely independent of the content and context of the investigation.

Probe Asking again in a deeper way during an interview.

Reliability One of the standard criteria in standardized/quantitative research, measured for example by repeating a test and assessing whether the results are the same in both cases.

Representativeness Either understood in a statistical way: is the population represented in the sample in the distribution of features (age, gender, employment, etc.)? Or in a theoretical way: are the study and its results covering the theoretically relevant aspects of the issue?

Research design A systematic plan for a research project, including who to integrate in the research (sampling), who or what to compare for which dimensions, etc.

Research diaries The researchers continuously note their impressions and what happens during field contacts or in preparing the study, or during analysis of the data.

Research perspectives Major approaches in qualitative research, under which the variety of methods can be summarized.

Research program An approach that includes more than a method, such as a concept of reality, an overall strategy, a specific tradition, etc.

Research proposal Research plan developed for applying for funding or in a PhD or master's program.

Research question What is it exactly that you want to find out?

Rigour Degree of consistency and consequence in applying a method or in doing an analysis.

Sampling Selection of cases or materials for the study from a larger population or variety of possibilities.

Shortcut strategies Pragmatic ways of using specific methods in situations of applied research, where it may be difficult to use these methods in their full versions (for example, in the context of qualitative evaluation).

Site Specific field for studying a process or issue in general, such as an institution, a community, an area, etc.

Social representation A concept for describing the knowledge of social groups about scientific findings or other issues.

Standardization The degree of controlling a research situation by defining and delimiting as many features of it as are necessary or possible.

Standards for qualitative research Attempts to define minimal requirements of quality or common procedures to apply in any form of qualitative research.

Strategic sampling A more directed way of selecting cases and examples in ethnographic research.

Substantive theory A more specific theory (in grounded theory research) referring to one area.

Symbolic interactionism A background theory in qualitative research based on the assumption that people act and interact on the basis of the meaning of objects and their interpretation.

Theoretical sampling The sampling procedure in grounded theory research, where cases, groups or materials are sampled according to their relevance for the theory that is developed and on the background of what is already the state of knowledge after collecting and analyzing a certain number of cases.

Transcription Transformation of recorded materials (conversations, interviews, visual materials, etc.) into text in order to analyze it.

Transparency The degree of how far a reader of a research study is enabled to understand how the research went on in concrete terms.

Triangulation The combination of different methods, theories, data and/or researchers in the study of one issue.

Tuskegee Syphilis Study An experiment in which a population of people infected with syphilis were neither informed about their illness nor given any treatment in order to study the uninfluenced course of this disease.

Validity One of the standard criteria in standardized/quantitative research, analyzed for example by looking for confounding influences (internal validity) or for transferability to situations beyond the current research situation (external validity).

Vulnerable population People in a specific situation (social discrimination, risks, illness) that makes a specific sensitiveness necessary when studying them.

‖ References

Angrosino, M. (2007) *Doing Ethnographic and Observational Research* (Book 3 of *The SAGE Qualitative Research Kit*). London: Sage.

Banks, M. (2007) *Using Visual Data in Qualitative Research* (Book 5 of *The SAGE Qualitative Research Kit*). London: Sage.

Bannister, P., Burman, E., Parker, I., Taylor, M. and Tindall, C. (1994) *Qualitative Methods in Psychology – A Practical Guide*. Buckingham: Open University Press.

Barbour, R. (2001) 'Checklists for improving rigour in qualitative research: a case of the tail wagging the dog?', *British Medical Journal*, 322: 1115–17.

Barbour, R. (2007) *Doing Focus Groups* (Book 4 of *The SAGE Qualitative Research Kit*). London: Sage.

Becker, H.S. (1967) 'Whose side are we on?', *Social Problems*, 14: 239–47.

Becker, H.S., Geer, B., Hughes, E.C. and Strauss, A.L. (1961) *Boys in White: Student Culture in Medical School*. Chicago: University of Chicago Press.

Berger, P.L. and Luckmann, T. (1966) *The Social Construction of Reality*. Garden City, NY: Doubleday.

Bryman, A. (1992) 'Quantitative and qualitative research: further reflections on their integration', in J. Brannen (ed.), *Mixing Methods: Quantitative and Qualitative Research*. Aldershot: Avebury, pp. 57–80.

Bryman, A. (2004) *Social Research Methods* (2nd ed.). Oxford: Oxford University Press.

Charmaz, K. (2006) *Constructing Grounded Theory – A Practical Guide Through Qualitative Analysis*. Thousand Oaks, CA: Sage.

Christian, C.G. (2005) 'Ethics and politics in qualitative research', in N. Denzin and Y.S. Lincoln (eds), *The Sage Handbook of Qualitative Research* (3rd ed.). Thousand Oaks, CA: Sage, pp. 139–64.

Clifford, J. and Marcus, G.E. (eds) (1986) *Writing Culture: The Poetics and Politics of Ethnography*. Berkeley: University of California Press.

Creswell, J.W. (1998) *Qualitative Inquiry and Research Design – Choosing among Five Traditions*. Thousand Oaks, CA: Sage.

Creswell, J.W. (2003) *Research Design – Qualitative, Quantitative and Mixed Methods Approaches* (2nd ed.). Thousand Oaks, CA: Sage.

Crossley, M. (2003) '"Would you consider yourself a healthy person?" Using focus groups to explore health as a moral phenomenon', *Journal of Health Psychology*, 8(5): 501–14.

Denzin, N.K. (1989) *The Research Act* (3rd ed.). Englewood Cliffs, NJ: Prentice-Hall.

Denzin, N.K. (2004) 'Reading film: using photos and video as social science material', in U. Flick, E. von Kardorff and I. Steinke (eds), *A Companion to Qualitative Research*. London: Sage, pp. 234–47.

Denzin, N. and Lincoln, Y.S. (eds) (1994) *Handbook of Qualitative Research*. London: Sage.

Denzin, N. and Lincoln, Y.S. (eds) (2000) *Handbook of Qualitative Research* (2nd ed.). London: Sage.

Denzin, N. and Lincoln, Y.S. (2005a) 'Introduction: the discipline and practice of qualitative research', in N. Denzin and Y.S. Lincoln (eds), *The Sage Handbook of Qualitative Research* (3rd ed.). Thousand Oaks, CA: Sage, pp. 1–32.

Denzin, N. and Lincoln, Y.S. (eds) (2005b) *The Sage Handbook of Qualitative Research* (3rd ed.). Thousands Oaks, CA: Sage.

Denzin, N. and Lincoln, Y.S. (2005c) 'Preface', in N. Denzin and Y.S. Lincoln (eds), *The Sage Handbook of Qualitative Research* (3rd ed.). Thousand Oaks, CA: Sage, pp. ix–xix.

Fleck, C. (2004) 'Marie Jahoda', in U. Flick, E. von Kardorff and I. Steinke (eds), *A Companion to Qualitative Research*. London: Sage, pp. 58–62.

Flick, U. (ed.) (1998a) *Psychology of the Social: Representations in Knowledge and Language*. Cambridge: Cambridge University Press.

Flick, U. (1998b) 'The social construction of individual and public health: contributions of social representations theory to a social science of health', *Social Science Information*, 37: 639–62.

Flick, U. (2000a) 'Qualitative inquiries into social representations of health', *Journal of Health Psychology*, 5: 309–18.

Flick, U. (2000b) 'Episodic interviewing', in M. Bauer and G. Gaskell (eds), *Qualitative Researching with Text, Image and Sound: A Handbook*. London: Sage, pp. 75–92.

Flick, U. (ed.) (2002) *Innovation durch New Public Health*. Göttingen: Hogrefe.

Flick, U. (2004a) 'Design and process in qualitative research', in U. Flick, E. von Kardorff and I. Steinke (eds), *A Companion to Qualitative Research*. London: Sage, pp. 146–52.

Flick, U. (2004b) 'Constructivism', in U. Flick, E. von Kardorff and I. Steinke (eds), *A Companion to Qualitative Research*. London: Sage, pp. 88–94.

Flick, U. (2006) *An Introduction to Qualitative Research* (3rd ed.). London: Sage.

Flick, U. (2007) *Managing Quality in Qualitative Research* (Book 8 of *The SAGE Qualitative Research Kit*). London: Sage.

Flick, U. and Foster, J. (2007) 'Social representations', in C. Willig and W. Stainton-Rogers (eds), *The SAGE Handbook of Qualitative Research in Psychology*. London: Sage (in press).

Flick, U., Fischer, C., Walter, U. and Schwartz F.W. (2002) 'Social representations of health held by health professionals – the case of general practitioners and home care nurses', *Social Science Information*, 41(4): 581–602.

Flick, U., Fischer, C., Neuber, A., Walter, U. and Schwartz, F.W. (2003) 'Health in the context of being old – representations held by health professionals', *Journal of Health Psychology*, 8(5): 539–56.

Flick, U. and Röhnsch, G. (2007) 'Idealism and neglect: health concept of homeless adolescents', *Journal of Health Psychology*, 12(5), in press.

Flick, U., Kardorff, E. von and Steinke, I. (eds) (2004a) *A Companion to Qualitative Research*. London: Sage.

Flick, U., Kardorff, E. von and Steinke, I. (2004b) 'What is qualitative research – introduction and overview', in U. Flick, E. von Kardorff and I. Steinke (eds), *A Companion to Qualitative Research*. London: Sage, pp. 3–12.

Frank, A.W. (1995). *Wounded Storyteller: Body, Illness, and Ethics*. Chicago: University of Chicago Press.

Gergen, K.J. (1999) *An Invitation to Social Construction*. London: Sage.

Gibbs, G. R. (2007) *Analyzing Qualitative Data* (Book 6 of *The SAGE Qualitative Research Kit*). London: Sage.

Glaser, B.G. (1992) *Basics of Grounded Theory Analysis: Emergence vs. Forcing*. Mill Valley, CA: Sociology Press.

References

Glaser, B.G. and Strauss, A.L. (1965) *Awareness of Dying*. Chicago: Aldine.

Glaser, B.G. and Strauss, A.L. (1967) *The Discovery of Grounded Theory: Strategies for Qualitative Research*. New York: Aldine.

Glasersfeld, E. von (1995) *Radical Constructivism: A Way of Knowing and Learning*. London: Falmer Press.

Goffman, E. (1959) *The Presentation of Self in Everyday Life*. New York: Doubleday.

Hammersley, M. (1995) *The Politics of Social Research*. London: Sage.

Hammersley, M. (1996) 'The relationship between qualitative and quantitative research: paradigm loyalty versus methodological eclecticism', in J.T.E. Richardson (ed.), *Handbook of Qualitative Research Methods for Psychology and the Social Sciences*. Leicester: BPS Books, pp. 159–74.

Hammersley, M. and Atkinson. P. (1995) *Ethnography: Principles in Practice* (2nd ed.). London: Routledge.

Hitzler, R. and Eberle, T.S. (2004) 'Phenomenological analysis of lifeworlds', in U. Flick, E. von Kardorff and I. Steinke (eds), *A Companion to Qualitative Research*. London: Sage, pp. 67–71.

Hochschild, A.R. (1983) *The Managed Heart*. Berkeley: University of California Press.

Hopf, C. (2004) 'Research ethics and qualitative research: an overview', in U. Flick, E. von Kardorff and I. Steinke (eds), *A Companion to Qualitative Research*. London. Sage, pp. 334–9.

Humphreys, L. (1975) *Tearoom Trade: Impersonal Sex in Public Places* (enlarged ed.). New York: Aldine.

Jahoda, M. (1995) 'Jahoda, M., Lazarsfeld, P. & Zeisel, H.: Die Arbeitslosen von Marienthal', in U. Flick, E. von Kardorff, H. Keupp, L. von Rosenstiel and S. Wolff (eds), *Handbuch Qualitative Sozialforschung* (2nd ed.). München: Psychologie Verlags Union, pp. 119–22.

Jahoda, M., Lazarsfeld, P.F. and Zeisel, H. (1933/1971) *Marienthal: The Sociology of an Unemployed Community*. Chicago: Aldine-Atherton.

Kelle, U. and Erzberger, C. (2004) 'Quantitative and qualitative methods: no confrontation', in U. Flick, E. von Kardorff and I. Steinke (eds), *A Companion to Qualitative Research*. London: Sage, pp. 172–7.

Knoblauch, H., Flick, U. and Maeder, C. (eds), 'The state of the art of qualitative research in Europe', special issue of *Forum Qualitative Social Research – FQS*, 6(3) (2005) (http://www.qualitative-research.net/fqs/fqs-e/inhalt3-05-e.htm).

Knorr-Cetina, K. (1981) *The Manufacture of Knowledge: An Essay on the Constructivist and Contextual Nature of Science*. Oxford: Pergamon Press.

Kvale, S. (2007) *Doing Interviews* (Book 2 of *The SAGE Qualitative Research Kit*). London: Sage.

Lincoln, Y.S. and Guba, E.G. (1985) *Naturalistic Inquiry*. London: Sage.

Lofland, J. (1976) *Doing Social Life: The Qualitative Study of Human Interaction in Natural Settings*. New York: Wiley.

Lüders, C. (1995) 'Von der Teilnehmenden Beobachtung zur ethnographischen Beschreibung – Ein Literaturbericht', in E. König and P. Zedler (eds), *Bilanz qualitativer Forschung*, Vol. 1. Weinheim: Deutscher Studienverlag, pp. 311–42.

Lüders, C. (2004a) 'The challenges of qualitative research', in U. Flick, E. von Kardorff and I. Steinke (eds), *A Companion to Qualitative Research*. London: Sage, pp. 359–64.

Lüders, C. (2004b) 'Field observation and ethnography', in U. Flick, E. von Kardorff and I. Steinke (eds), *A Companion to Qualitative Research*. London: Sage, pp. 222–30.

Lüders, C. and Reichertz, J. (1986) 'Wissenschaftliche Praxis ist, wenn alles funktioniert und keiner weiß warum: Bemerkungen zur Entwicklung qualitativer Sozialforschung', *Sozialwissenschaftliche Literaturrundschau*, 12: 90–102.

References

Marcus, G. (1995) 'Ethnography in/of the world system: the emergence of multi-sited ethnography' *Annual Review of Anthropology*, 24: 95–117.

Marshall, C. and Rossman, G.B. (2006) *Designing Qualitative Research* (4th ed.). Thousand Oaks, CA: Sage.

Maxwell, J.A. (2005) *Qualitative Research Design – An Interactive Approach* (2nd ed.). Thousand Oaks, CA: Sage.

Merkens, H. (2004) 'Selection procedures, sampling, case construction', in U. Flick, E. von Kardorff and I. Steinke (eds), *A Companion to Qualitative Research*. London, Sage, pp. 165–71.

Miles, M.B. and Huberman, A.M. (1994) *Qualitative Data Analysis: A Sourcebook of New Methods* (2nd ed.). Newbury Park, CA: Sage.

Morse, J.M. (1994) 'Designing funded qualitative research', in N.K. Denzin and Y. S. Lincoln (eds), *Handbook of Qualitative Research*. Thousand Oaks, CA: Sage, pp. 220–35.

Moscovici, S. (1973) 'Foreword', in C. Herzlich, *Health and Illness: A Social Psychological Analysis*. London: Academic Press.

Moscovici, S. (1998) 'The history and actuality of social representations', in U. Flick (ed.), *The Psychology of the Social*. Cambridge: Cambridge University Press, pp. 209–47.

Oakley, A. (1999) 'People's ways of knowing: gender and methodology', in S. Hood, B. Mayall and S. Olivier (eds), *Critical Issues in Social Research: Power and Prejudice*. Buckingham: Open University Press, pp. 154–70.

Patton, M.Q. (2002) *Qualitative Evaluation and Research Methods* (3rd ed.). London: Sage.

Puchta, C. and Potter, J. (2004) *Focus Group Practice*. London: Sage.

Punch, M. (1994) 'Politics and ethics in qualitative research', in N. Denzin and Y.S. Lincoln (eds), *Handbook of Qualitative Research*. Thousand Oaks, CA: Sage, pp. 83–97.

Ragin, C.C. (1994) *Constructing Social Research*. Thousand Oaks, CA: Pine Forge Press.

Ragin, C.C. and Becker, H.S. (eds) (1992) *What Is a Case? Exploring the Foundations of Social Inquiry*. Cambridge: Cambridge University Press.

Rapley, T. (2007) *Doing Conversation, Discourse and Document Analysis* (Book 7 of *The SAGE Qualitative Research Kit*). London: Sage.

Rosenthal, G. and Fischer-Rosenthal, W. (2004) 'The analysis of biographical-narrative interviews', in U. Flick, E. von Kardorff and I. Steinke (eds), *A Companion to Qualitative Research*. London: Sage, pp. 259–65.

Rubin, H.J. and Rubin, I.S. (1995) *Qualitative Interviewing*. Thousand Oaks, CA: Sage.

Rubin, H.J. and Rubin, I.S. (2005) *Qualitative Interviewing* (2nd ed.). Thousand Oaks, CA: Sage.

Schütz, A. (1962) *Collected Papers*, Vols I and II. Den Haag: Nijhoff.

Schwartz, F.W. (ed.) (2003) *Das Public Health Buch* (2nd ed.). München: Urban & Fischer.

Seale, C. (1999) *The Quality of Qualitative Research*. London: Sage.

Seale, C., Gobo, G., Gubrium, J. and Silverman, D. (2004) (eds) *Qualitative Research Practice*. London: Sage.

Silverman, D. (2006) *Interpreting Qualitative Data* (3rd ed.). London: Sage.

Smith, J.A. (2003) (ed.) *Qualitative Psychology: A Practical Guide to Research Methods*. London: Sage.

Tashakkori, A. and Teddlie, C. (eds) (2003a) *Handbook of Mixed Methods in Social and Behavioral Research*. Thousand Oaks, CA: Sage.

Tashakkori, A. and Teddlie, C. (2003b) 'Major issues and controversies in the use of mixed methods in social and behavioral research', in A. Tashakkori and C. Teddlie (eds), *Handbook of Mixed Methods in Social and Behavioral Research*. Thousand Oaks, CA: Sage, pp. 3–50.

References

ten Have, P. (1999) *Doing Conversation Analysis: A Practical Guide*. London: Sage.

Thomson, R., Plumridge, L. and Holland, J. (eds) (2003) 'Longitudinal qualitative research', *Special issue of the International Journal of Social Research Methodology – Theory and Practice,* 6(3).

van Maanen, J. (1988) *Tales of the Field: On Writing Ethnography*. Chicago: University of Chicago Press.

Vidich, A.J. and Lyman, S.M. (2000) 'Qualitative methods: their history in sociology and anthropology', in N.K. Denzin and Y.S. Lincoln (eds), *Handbook of Qualitative Research* (2nd ed.). Thousand Oaks, CA: Sage, pp. 37–84.

Wilkinson, S. (1998) 'Focus group methodology: a review', *International Journal of Social Research Methodology,* 1(3): 181–203.

Willig, C. and Stainton-Rogers, W. (eds) (2007) *The SAGE Handbook of Qualitative Research in Psychology*. London: Sage (in press).

Wolff, S. (2004) 'Ways into the field and their variants', in U. Flick, E. von Kardorff and I. Steinke (eds), *A Companion to Qualitative Research*. London: Sage, pp. 195–202.

▌▌ Author index

▌▌▌ Subject index